YEMEN
ON THE BRINK

YEMEN
ON THE BRINK

CHRISTOPHER BOUCEK AND **MARINA OTTAWAY**, EDITORS

CARNEGIE ENDOWMENT
FOR INTERNATIONAL PEACE

WASHINGTON DC ▪ MOSCOW ▪ BEIJING ▪ BEIRUT ▪ BRUSSELS

Carnegie Endowment for International Peace
1779 Massachusetts Avenue, N.W., Washington, D.C. 20036
202-483-7600 www.ceip.org

To order, contact Carnegie's distributor:
Hopkins Fulfillment Service
PO Box 50370, Baltimore, MD 21211-4370
1-800-537-5487 or 1-410-516-6956
Fax: 1-410-516-6998

Library of Congress Cataloging-in-Publication Data

Yemen on the brink / Christopher Boucek and Marina Ottaway, editors.
   p. cm.
   Includes index.
   ISBN 978-0-87003-253-0 (pbk.) – ISBN 978-0-87003-254-7 (cloth) 1. Yemen (Republic)–Politics and government. 2. Political violence–Yemen (Republic) 3. Islamic fundamentalism–Yemen (Republic) 4. Qaida (Organization) I. Boucek, Christopher. II. Ottaway, Marina.

JQ1842.A58Y46 2010
953.305'3–dc22   2010017143

Cover design by Zeena Feldman
Composition by Oakland Street Publishing
Printed by United Book Press

CONTENTS

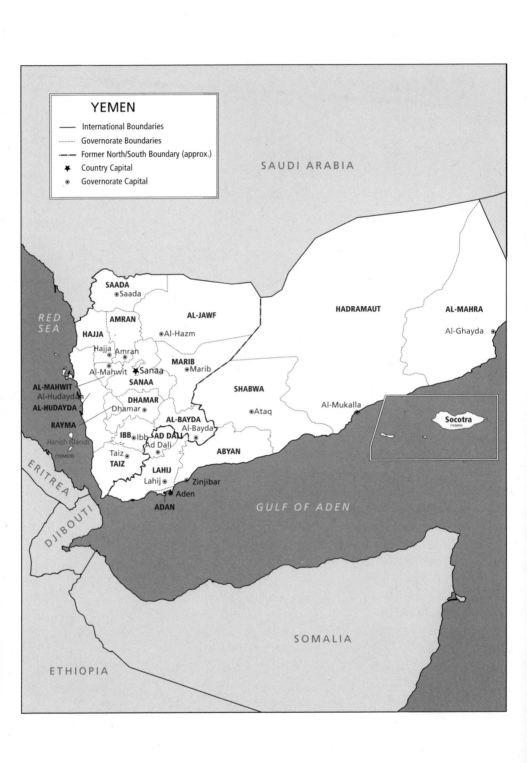

YEMEN

— International Boundaries
········· Governorate Boundaries
—·—·— Former North/South Boundary (approx.)
✹ Country Capital
◉ Governorate Capital

SAUDI ARABIA

RED
SEA

SAADA
◉ Saada

AL-JAWF

HADRAMAUT

AL-MAHRA

AMRAN

HAJJA

◉ Al-Hazm

Al-Ghayda ◉

Hajja Amran

Al-Mahwit   ✹ Sanaa

MARIB
◉ Marib

SANAA

AL-MAHWIT
Al-Hudaydah

DHAMAR

SHABWA

AL-HUDAYDA

Dhamar ◉

◉ Ataq

Al-Mukalla

Socotra
(YEMEN)

RAYMA

AL-BAYDA
Al-Bayda

Hanish Islands
(YEMEN)

IBB
◉ Ibb

AD DALI
Ad Dali

Taiz ◉

ABYAN

TAIZ

ERITREA

LAHIJ

Lahij ◉   ◉ Zinjibar

◉ Aden

DJIBOUTI

ADAN

GULF OF ADEN

SOMALIA

ETHIOPIA

FOREWORD

Yemen faces an alarming confluence of challenges to its stability and that of its neighbors, and poses a real threat to the security of countries as far away as the United States. Dire economic circumstances, including poverty, unemployment, inflation, and the depletion of natural resources are compounded by the country's addiction to qat—a widely produced and consumed stimulant—as well as the serious security threats of smuggling, religious and tribal conflict, terrorism, and war. Yemen has them all.

This volume presents groundbreaking new analysis of Yemen's most pressing concerns, for the benefit of Western policy makers and other readers who recognize how dramatically the country's condition could affect them if it continues to deteriorate. Christopher Boucek, who warned of the country's dangerous downward spiral in September 2009, provides a broad overview of Yemen's deterioration and examines in detail the six rounds of fighting in Saada province. Sarah Phillips explores Yemen's tribal dynamics and the limits of foreign intervention in the country's problems. Stephen Day assesses the southern secessionist movement and support for al-Qaeda in the Arabian Peninsula (AQAP). Alistair Harris provides insights into whether the Yemeni regime can address the grievances articulated and tapped into by AQAP. In the concluding chapter Boucek and co-author Marina Ottaway reflect on the options available to the international community to help stabilize the country.

The Republic of Yemen is strategically located between Saudi Arabia and Somalia—part of two distinct, yet interconnected regions, the Arabian Peninsula and the Horn of Africa. Though the country has been excluded from the wealthy Gulf Cooperation Council, it is in many ways more able to withstand multiple challenges than its East African neighbors. More than 3 million barrels of oil pass Yemen's coast every day, through treacherous waters where Islamist terrorists and Somali pirates have staged many successful maritime attacks disrupting international commerce and the flow of vital hydrocarbons.

Inside Yemen, Islamist terrorists threaten Yemen's domestic security, in the form of a resurgent al-Qaeda organization, as do an increasingly active secessionist movement in the South, and the armed insurrection in the North. While Yemen has survived crises in the past, they have tended to be singular events. The many problems Yemen now suffers are unprecedented in range and scope, and a historical absence of much central control makes it even more difficult to build effective national government.

As severe as these security challenges are, at the heart of Yemen's problems is a looming economic crisis. The country is the poorest in the Arab world, its oil reserves are fast running out, and it has few viable options for a sustainable post-oil economy. Moreover, it is consuming its limited water resources much faster than it can replenish them. An impoverished and rapidly expanding population places unbearable pressure on the government, which can scarcely provide basic services. The faltering economy and poorly prepared workforce have pushed unemployment to 35 percent, on par with the Great Depression in the United States. Even for those who find work, poverty remains severe. The country has an annual per capita income of under $900, and nearly half the population earns less than $2 per day.

Yemen also confronts staggering demographic challenges. Though the population growth rate has decreased slightly in the past decade, it remains among the highest in the world, at just over 3.4 percent per year. As a result, more than two-thirds of the Yemeni people are under the age of 24, more than half of them illiterate. In the next two decades, Yemeni and Western analysts expect the country's population to nearly double to more than 40 million.

The difficult terrain and geographic dispersion of the population exacerbate the demographic challenges. Yemen's 23 million people are spread throughout roughly 135,000 villages and settlements. Many Yemeni villages are remote, spread across mountainsides and desert wadis, with less than one-third of the population living in urban areas. The central government has been unable to extend either a government presence or more than the most basic social services to its people. As a result, many settlements are forced to provide their own health care, schools, and other social

services. The central government already struggles to exert control throughout the country, and its situation will only worsen as time passes.

In short, Yemen embodies a perfect storm of domestic and international
challenges, and while they are all interrelated, any useful analysis—the
starting point for addressing them—must break them down into manageable chunks. This book is a valuable start.

Jessica T. Mathews
President, Carnegie Endowment for International Peace

YEMEN: AVOIDING A DOWNWARD SPIRAL

Christopher Boucek

Yemen is beset by a host of challenges that endanger both its domestic stability and regional security. The United States and the international community must act now, before conditions deteriorate further, to help Yemen meet these challenges. While Yemen has survived crises in the past, they have tended to be singular events, while the many problems it now faces are unprecedented in range and scope.

The problems include international terrorism, violent extremism, religious and tribal conflict, separatism, and transnational smuggling. Attempts to build effective national governance are frustrated by porous borders, a heavily armed population, and a historical absence of much central government control. Between Saudi Arabia and Somalia, Yemen is strategically located—part of two different yet interconnected regions, the Arabian Peninsula and the Horn of Africa. This fact often frustrates policy analyses; Yemen is excluded from the wealthy Gulf Cooperation Council, but is in many ways more resilient than its East African neighbors. More than 3 million barrels of oil pass through the treacherous waters off the country's coast every day. The constant risk of attack by Islamist terrorists and Somali pirates threatens to disrupt the flow of vital hydrocarbons and international commerce more broadly.

Interrelated economic, demographic, and domestic security challenges are converging to threaten the stability of Yemen. At the heart of the country's problems is a looming economic crisis. Yemen's oil reserves are fast running out, with few viable options for a sustainable post-oil economy. Moreover, the country's limited water resources are being consumed much

1

faster than they are being replenished. A rapidly expanding and increasingly poorer population places unbearable pressure on the government's ability to provide basic services. Domestic security is endangered by Islamist terrorism, magnified by a resurgent al-Qaeda organization, an armed insurrection in the North, and an increasingly active secessionist movement in the South.

These challenges are compounded by corruption and an absence of central government control in much of the country, as well as by the pending transition in political leadership. President Ali Abdullah Saleh has ruled the Republic of Yemen since the unification of the Yemen Arab Republic in the North and the People's Democratic Republic of Yemen in the South in 1990. The next presidential election is scheduled for 2013. It is unclear whether Saleh will be eligible to stand for re-election for what would be a third term, and he has no obvious successor. The post-Saleh government will be severely strained by a combination of reduced revenue and diminished state capacity.

Yemen is the poorest country in the Arab world, and its population growth rate, which exceeds 3 percent per year, is among the world's highest. The government has been unable to provide adequate educational or other public services for the rapidly expanding population, more than two-thirds of which is under the age of 24, and illiteracy stands at over 50 percent. The faltering economy and poorly prepared workforce have pushed unemployment to 35 percent, on par with the Great Depression in the United States. The country's dire economic circumstances will soon limit the government's ability to deliver the funds needed to hold the country together. The population is expected to double to 40 million over the next two decades, by which time Yemen will no longer be an oil producer, and its water resources will be severely diminished.

Yemen has been frequently discussed by observers as a failing state, and with good reason. Owing to the central government's weak control, the country has often been on the brink of chaos, yet it has always managed to muddle through. One of its crises was precipitated by the Saleh regime's failure to support United Nations Security Council resolutions calling for the use of force to evict Iraqi troops from Kuwait in 1990. U.S., Western, and Gulf Arab aid was cut dramatically in retaliation, and nearly 1 million Yemeni workers were expelled from Saudi Arabia. The unification of North and South Yemen earlier in 1990 and the 1994 civil war in which the South attempted to secede have also presented major challenges for the central government. However, unlike these individual challenges, the problems facing the country today are multiple and interconnected, each one posing serious threats to the future of Yemen, and together potentially overwhelming the state's limited capacity.

Any single event—or more likely a confluence of worst-case events beyond the ability of the Yemeni government to control—could lead to a further erosion of central government authority in Yemen and destabilization of the region. A major humanitarian crisis, triggered perhaps by severe famine or crop failure, could, for instance, result in a large refugee emergency in which the government would be unable to provide even rudimentary relief services. A balance-of-payments crisis in which the regime could no longer afford to placate the urban areas that receive government services would be disastrous. An inability of a post-Saleh president to balance Yemen's competing interests and stakeholders could create a power vacuum, with separate regions possibly growing more autonomous and independent from the central government in Sanaa.

Still, Yemen boasts a relatively resilient society that has already endured much, with little assistance from Sanaa. In some regards, in fact, low expectations for the Yemeni government to deal with future crises may help lessen their potential impact. Because rural *muhafazat*, or governorates, the administrative divisions in Yemen, do not currently rely on Sanaa for goods and services, what happens at the national level in the future may make little difference to much of the population.

If, however, the central government's authority and legitimacy continue to deteriorate, Yemen may slowly devolve into semi-autonomous regions and cities. This trajectory has occurred in other countries, such as Somalia and Afghanistan, with disastrous consequences. Such a slow, emerging state of semi-lawlessness in Yemen would provide opportunities for extremists directed or inspired by al-Qaeda to regroup, organize, train, and launch operations against U.S. and allied targets throughout the Gulf region.

No perfect solutions exist for Yemen's problems today, and none of its many pressing challenges can be fully averted. Steps, however, can be taken to lessen their impact. The United States has a stake in helping Yemen deal with its problems; given the country's strategic importance to American national security interests and foreign policy objectives, the cost of inaction would be too great. Furthermore, failure to act now would lead to fewer and even worse options in the future.

Interlocking Challenges

Yemen's future lies at the intersection of three major interconnected challenges: economic, demographic, and domestic security.

Economic Challenges

Vital natural resource depletion, the effects of the global economic downturn, corruption, unemployment, and inflation pose the most significant long-term economic threats to the country. Yemen is the poorest country in the Arab world, and it is getting poorer because of government policies, complicated by rising prices and an inability to absorb a growing population into the domestic labor market.

RESOURCE DEPLETION: OIL. Oil exports, which generate more than 75 percent of government revenue, are absolutely critical for the Yemeni economy. The government relies on the hard currency provided by oil sales to fund state expenditures. More importantly, in the absence of mature and enduring state governance institutions, oil revenue helps to maintain extensive patronage networks that balance competing interests among various tribes and other stakeholders.

Rapidly decreasing oil reserves, however, coupled with a dramatic fall in global oil prices have had a severe impact on the Yemeni economy. Production is decreasing in both areas where Yemen's oil reserves are concentrated—the Marib basin in the middle of the country and the Masila basin in the East—as the fields approach the end of their useful cycles. Yemen's oil reserves are divided into 97 onshore and offshore exploration and production blocks, of which only twelve produce oil. The most significant of these are Marib (block 18), Masila (block 14), East Shabwa (block 10), Jannah (block 5), and West Iyad (block 4). British Petroleum has assessed Yemen's proved reserves at 2.8 billion barrels (the Yemeni government maintains that this figure grossly underestimates the reserves, but Sanaa's claims remain unsubstantiated).

Oil exports in Yemen have declined sharply in recent years, from more than 450,000 barrels per day at the peak in 2003 to roughly 280,000 barrels per day in January 2009, according to Amir Salem al-Aidroos, the minister of oil and minerals. Barring any major new discoveries, energy experts generously estimate that Yemen's oil exports will cease in ten years. The World Bank posits that by 2017 the government of Yemen will earn no income from oil. Other assessments suggest that the proved oil reserves will be exhausted in just five years. The true extent of the oil production decrease has been masked by recent high prices, which allowed Yemen to earn more money despite selling less crude oil. Since global prices have fallen from their summer 2008 record high, the country has been hit doubly hard—both in revenue per unit and total units sold. While falling reserves account for much of the drop in production, poor maintenance and limited capacity in Yemen's oil sector have exacerbated the problem.

The Ministry of Oil and Minerals has identified several obstacles to greater production, including the absence of a long-term strategic plan for the energy sector and the failure to streamline production sharing agreements. There are currently three separate agreements: one for oil, one for gas, and another for a combination of both. As a result, there is no incentive for oil companies to develop resources not covered under a production sharing agreement. Any gas found during oil exploration, for example, is not developed because it was not what the operating company was licensed to extract. Moreover, each individual production sharing agreement must go before parliament for approval before production may begin, leading to months-long delays in some cases. To address this, the ministry is seeking the authority to issue and approve future agreements. Separately, the ministry wants greater geological study, through the use of costly seismic and advanced imaging technologies, to detect hydrocarbon deposits. It is unclear, however, that even the most sophisticated analyses would discover more oil, and in any case, difficult physical and security conditions would complicate further extraction.

As a result of decreased oil export earnings, the Yemeni government has sharply curtailed income expectations. During July 2008, crude oil was at a record high price of $147 per barrel; during the first quarter of 2009, according to the Central Bank of Yemen, it averaged just $43 per barrel, and the U.S. Energy Information Administration has estimated that prices will average $55 per barrel for the second half of the year.

Further complicating the national budget, which is dependent on oil revenue, is that most of the budget, including government subsidies, salaries, and pensions, has traditionally been politically off-limits. In recognition of the severe budgetary shortfalls, at the beginning of 2009 the Finance Ministry reportedly ordered budget cuts of 50 percent throughout the entire bureaucracy; according to the Economist Intelligence Unit, however, cuts of only 4 percent have been implemented. Furthermore, these reductions have not been applied universally across the entire government; the Defense and Interior ministries, among others, will not be affected. In actuality, the financial straits are much more severe than had been predicted. Data released by the Central Bank of Yemen indicate that revenue from oil exports hit a record low in the first quarter of 2009, down 75 percent from the same period in 2008.

Clearly, Yemen's oil resources are running out, and finding new sources of oil reserves is not a feasible solution. Attempts to cut the budget, meanwhile, have not succeeded. It is imperative that the country prepare for a post-oil economy.

RESOURCE DEPLETION: WATER. While Yemen's dwindling oil reserves are a major concern, ultimately more worrisome is the rapidly depleting water supply. Shortages are acute throughout the country, and Sanaa, whose population is growing at 7 percent a year as a result of increased urbanization, may become the first capital city in the world to run out of water. This crisis is the result of several factors, including rising domestic consumption, poor water management, corruption, absence of resource governance, and wasteful irrigation techniques. Until five years ago, there was no Water and Environment Ministry, and today legal oversight remains limited. According to a 2009 UN Food and Agriculture Organization report, Yemen is among the world's most water-scarce nations, with one of the lowest rates of per capita fresh water availability. Because of an absence of any serious or enforceable legal oversight, water is being extracted from underground aquifers faster than it is being replaced. The water basin in Taiz, one of the largest cities, collapsed in 1998. Water extraction rates in Sanaa are now estimated at four times that of replenishment, and the basin there and in Amran are close to collapse, with the Saada basin estimated to follow shortly thereafter. According to one recent analysis, nineteen of the country's 21 aquifers are not being replenished.[1] In some cases, nonrenewable fossil water is now being extracted.

In recent years, the water table in Yemen has fallen about 2 meters, or 6.6 feet, per year, forcing wells to be dug deeper. This affects the quality of the water—the British think tank Chatham House noted in a sobering analysis that it is deteriorating because of increased concentration of minerals.[2] The falling water table also often necessitates the use of oil drilling rigs. While a legal regime now exists to assure the fair and equitable usage of surface water, there is no such legal regime for groundwater. As a result, anyone who wants water (and can afford to do so) digs a well and draws out as much water as possible. Abdul Rahman al-Iryani, the minister of water and environment, has estimated that 99 percent of all water extraction is unlicensed.

The importation of drill rigs is not subject to any customs duty, licensing process, or taxation. As of January 2009, Water and Environment Ministry officials estimate that more than 800 private drill rigs are operating in the country. In contrast, there are only three in all of Jordan, and India—whose population is more than 50 times that of Yemen—has just 100.

In an attempt to address the country's water crisis, the central government has sought to decentralize water and sanitation services, in essence making the governorates responsible for themselves. This effort fits within a larger government strategy of devolving control to local governorates to circumvent the fact that much of the territory of Yemen lies outside of central government control. According to al-Iryani, the water and environment minister, fifteen local water corporations have been created to manage local resources. Most of the country's major cities have been covered through this project, including Ibb, Taiz, Hodeida, Aden, Mukalla, Amran, Dhamar, and Sanaa city (administratively, the capital is differentiated from the surrounding governorate, also known as Sanaa). This is important because most of the central government's support comes from these urban areas. According to many observers, the Saleh regime prioritizes the delivery of services to urban areas at the expense of rural governorates. The failure to establish local water corporations in several governorates that historically have not received much support or social services from the central government, and where control is exercised largely by tribal authorities, has raised fear that a resurgent al-Qaeda may seek refuge. Local water corporations have not yet been created in Marib, Jouf, Shabwa, Sanaa, Mahra, and Mahwit governorates. The Water and Environment Ministry has also said that it is in the process of establishing a local water corporation in the northern Saada governorate, ostensibly as a means to advance security and stability amid an ongoing civil conflict. The central government has done little reconstruction work or social service provision there, however, and it is unclear how a local water corporation can be created while the military wages a fierce and often indiscriminate campaign against an increasingly resilient guerrilla movement.

In one bright spot on the water front, an underground water basin was discovered near Mukalla in mid-2009, and estimates suggest that it could supply the region with water for many years. Yemeni officials note that the water was found at depths in excess of 200 meters, or 656 feet, demonstrating the increasingly difficult task of finding freshwater. Much of the water will likely go to the agricultural sector, the biggest consumer in the country. Officials also warn that the new find must be protected from contamination from saltwater, sewage, and the overuse of fertilizers and pesticides.

THE IMPACT OF QAT. A large amount of Yemen's water consumption is devoted to the irrigation of qat, a semi-narcotic plant habitually chewed by an estimated 75 percent of Yemeni men. Nearly all social interactions in Yemen, from business to government, revolve around daily afternoon qat chews. While exact figures are difficult to come by, a majority of Yemen's arable land is devoted to qat cultivation.

Qat is an especially hardy plant that grows in areas where other crops such as coffee would not. It is favored by farmers for its ability to generate cash quickly; when they are in need of income, farmers simply turn on the taps to irrigate the fields. After just weeks of irrigation, qat leaves can be harvested nearly year-round for same-day sales. Furthermore, it is much more profitable than other crops, such as grapes or potatoes.

Because qat is more productive as it is given more water, there are no incentives to conserve water in irrigation. Farmers will therefore often over-irrigate their fields with little consideration given to the environmental aftereffects, including soil degradation caused by exhausting soil nutrients. The greatest expense for qat farmers is diesel to run the pumps to draw groundwater for their fields. In an example of Yemen's interconnected challenges, qat cultivation thus benefits indirectly from the government's diesel subsidies.

For all the problems associated with it, however, research has shown that there are also some beneficial aspects to qat cultivation by increasing the availability of local services and generating employment for rural Yemenis from other parts of the country. In an assessment of qat in Yemen, the World Bank noted that the qat trade facilitates regular transfers of money from cities to rural areas. Moreover, the vast majority of income from qat sales remains in the local area, and employment in qat cultivation helps to limit urbanization. Nonetheless, Yemen's qat habit has been identified as one of the main primary causes of poverty in the country, decreasing productivity, depleting scarce resources, and consuming an increasingly larger portion of household budgets.[3]

In fact, so much land is devoted to qat cultivation, which comprises a large part of the Yemeni economy, that the country's ability to grow its own food has decreased to the point that it is now a net food importer. Worse, more than 5 million Yemenis go hungry each day, according to the Ministry of Planning and International Cooperation, and the country's childhood malnutrition rates are among the highest in the world. The UN World Food Programme noted last year that 97 percent of Yemeni households surveyed did not have enough money to pay for food and other essentials, leading family members to forgo meals, reduce protein consumption, seek second jobs, and sell personal belongings in an effort to cope. In May 2009, the UN body said many Yemenis were down to just one meal per day. Two months later, it announced an urgent call for donors for food aid for at-risk groups, in particular women and children.

BROADER ECONOMIC WOES. Yemen suffers from the effects of the global economic downturn, endemic corruption, and inflation. Individually, each poses difficulties; together, they are a snapshot of an economy in crisis.

The downturn in the global economy has had a dire impact on Yemen. It has been hit hard by decreases in revenue and the dramatic fall in global crude oil prices. Critically, the global recession and economic slowdown in the Gulf have led to decreased remittances from Yemenis working abroad. Foreign investment, particularly from the Arab Gulf countries, is also down.

Corruption has also taken a toll. In recent years, Yemen has taken steps to curb corruption, enacting laws on money laundering, fiscal transparency, and anticorruption. Its Central Organization for Control and Auditing is recognized as an increasingly competent organization, and the establishment of the Supreme National Authority for Combating Corruption is a positive move, although the organization's impact will be limited until it is granted enforcement capabilities.

Yet despite these efforts, corruption continues to be a serious and continuing problem, and fair and transparent prosecutions are needed. The auditing agency has alleged that nearly 30 percent of government revenue is never deposited in government accounts. The U.S. Agency for International Development noted in its 2006 *Yemen Corruption Assessment* report that corruption in Yemen is a result of weak government institutions. It identified the four main sources of corruption as the national budgetary process; the procurement system; the military-commercial system; and the ruling General People's Congress, or GPC, party apparatus. Allegations of an active black-market trade in refined petroleum products, as well as officially sanctioned or tolerated smuggling, also persist.

The Yemeni economy has suffered from significant inflation for the past several years. Periodic—and often only temporary—decreases in government subsidies have contributed to rising consumer prices. Inflation reached 20 percent last year. It has recently been brought down closer to 12 percent; however, it is expected to go up again because of a cyclical rise in import prices anticipated in the next three years.

Demographic Challenges

A second major set of challenges confronting Yemen is demographic. Although the population growth rate has decreased slightly in recent years, it is among the highest in the world at just over 3.4 percent per year. As a result, more than two-thirds of the population is under the age of 24. In the next two decades, Yemeni and Western analysts alike expect Yemen's population to nearly double to more than 40 million people. Poverty is severe, with an annual per capita income of under $900 per year and nearly half the population earning less than $2 per day. Infant mortality is a major concern, in part a result of extremely limited pre- and postnatal care. Small programs established by European donors have had some success in combating this problem, but Yemeni children continue to die from preventable childhood illnesses.

Yemen's demographic challenges are exacerbated by the geographic dispersion of its population and the country's difficult terrain. Less than one-third of the population lives in urban areas—the rest is spead throughout roughly 135,000 remote villages and settlements. With so many of its people living on mountainsides and desert wadis, the central government has not been able to provide more than the most basic social services and is largely absent in these remote areas. As a result, the populations of many settlements are forced to be largely self-sufficient, often providing their own health care centers, schools, and other social services. In the future, the ability of the central government to effectively exert its control throughout the entire country and provide basic services is in serious doubt, as the population continues to rapidly expand.

EDUCATION. An inadequate education system aggravates the demographic challenges. The national literacy rate is about 50 percent, with female illiteracy near 70 percent. Women experience disproportionate difficulty in accessing education, with enrollment rates dropping off by half from primary to secondary school.

According to Minister of Education Abdulsalam al-Joufi, one of Yemen's greatest problems is an insufficient number of qualified teachers. At unification in 1990, more than half of the country's teachers were deemed to be unqualified. For a number of years after unification, the government virtually ceded control of the education system to religious conservatives. The government has since sought to regain control of the education system and introduce modest reforms. As of January 2009, there were 42 programs in place to retrain more than 90,000 teachers. Population growth in the years since 1990 has further strained the education system. There are now only about 16,000 schools for the 135,000 villages and settlements.

Among the efforts to improve the education system, the government has tried consolidating the state schools, independent Islamic schools, and the old socialist school system from the former South Yemen. Another step has been to standardize the curriculum to promote the teaching of a range of core subjects. In May 2009, the *Yemen Observer* reported that a new review would be conducted jointly by the ministries of Education and Religious Endowment and Islamic Affairs to evaluate the curriculum used in the estimated 4,500 religious schools in the country, all of which are ostensibly under some form of government supervision. Details of this oversight, however, remain lacking. Similarly, the discussion of politics in classrooms is officially forbidden by the ministry, and school principals are expected to monitor such activities and reprimand noncompliant teachers. This process, however, has also proven difficult to implement, and it is unclear what measures are available to remove problematic teachers.

Underregulated religious education has been a recurrent problem in Yemen. According to al-Joufi, all "scientific institutes"—a "parallel and separate" Islamist education system, largely funded from Saudi Arabia and focused on religious and Arabic language instruction[4]—were closed by the government, although several Western analysts doubt this assertion. As part of an effort to reassert the ministry's primacy, the building that previously housed the Sanaa Institute, once the country's largest extra-governmental institute, is now the headquarters of the Education Ministry. Nevertheless, teachers formerly employed at scientific institutes remain in Yemen, and many are still teaching.

The Yemeni government is carrying out a fifteen-year plan to address deficiencies in the education system. Current priorities include efforts to improve the overall quality, unify the curriculum, and increase girls' access to education. Despite limited resources, the Ministry of Education has additional goals to amalgamate and harmonize the national education system into one coherent body, increase supervision throughout schools, and implement a nationwide testing system. Throughout all these programs, the ministry is also seeking to recast the learning process away from rote memorization, the traditional model in Yemen.

EMPLOYMENT. More than 25,000 people enter the labor market each year, and the figure is increasing as Yemen's population rapidly expands. Because of the weak economy and lack of development, unemployment is conservatively estimated at 35 percent. Yemeni officials recognize that the central government is not able to hire all those seeking work and the private sector is unable to pick up the slack. Ali Mohammed al-Anisi, the director of the Presidential Office and chairman of the National Security Bureau, observes that unemployed youth are exploited by extremist elements, including al-Qaeda and Houthi rebels. The government acknowledges that the country's economic difficulties contribute to its security problems, and some officials recognize that the government's plans for addressing these issues are inadequate.

With Yemen's population set to double by 2030, the increase cannot be absorbed solely into the domestic labor market. Yemen will need to export labor to wealthy Gulf states. Labor remittances already contribute approximately $1 billion to the economy each year. The typical Yemeni expatriate worker supports up to seven people back home. However, Saudi Arabia and the other Gulf countries are no longer much interested in importing unskilled Yemeni laborers and it is unlikely that Yemeni workers will displace other third country nationals laboring in the Gulf. To be competitive, Yemen will need to export semiskilled workers, trained and certified in specialized areas. Toward this end, several regional states have launched training programs, and in July 2009, Saudi Arabia announced its intention to finance 69 technical training institutes in Yemen.

Domestic Security Challenges

The third major set of challenges facing Yemen involves domestic security. Counterterrorism and security concerns are the greatest immediate worries of U.S. and Western officials; in fact, without the fear of terrorism, it is doubtful that developments in Yemen would evoke much alarm in Western policy circles. The major domestic security threats are violent Islamist terrorism; the ongoing conflict in the northern province of Saada; the southern separatist movement; and piracy and border security. These issues all coalesce around a larger fear that a resurgent al-Qaeda will exploit the central government's weakness and will coalesce in under-governed spaces in Yemen to destabilize the region, mounting attacks against U.S. and other Western targets throughout the Gulf.

ISLAMIST EXTREMISM. Islamist extremism in Yemen is the result of a long and complicated set of developments. A large number of Yemeni nationals participated in the anti-Soviet jihad in Afghanistan during the 1980s. After the Soviet occupation ended, the Yemeni government encouraged its citizens to return and also permitted foreign veterans to settle in Yemen. Many of these Arab Afghans were co-opted by the regime and integrated into the state's various security apparatuses. Such co-optation was also used with individuals detained by the Yemeni government after the September 11 terrorist attacks. As early as 1993, the U.S. State Department noted in a now-declassified intelligence report that Yemen was becoming an important stop for many fighters leaving Afghanistan. The report also maintained that the Yemeni government was either unwilling or unable to curb their activities. Islamism and Islamist activists were used by the regime throughout the 1980s and 1990s to suppress domestic opponents, and during the 1994 civil war Islamists fought against southern forces. More recently, similar allegations were made that Islamist fighters have fought on behalf of the government in Saada and against southern separatists. While Islamists of various stripes may have fought in either theater, there is no evidence to suggest that al-Qaeda operatives have fought on behalf of the government.

After several serious terrorist attacks in the early 2000s, such as on the USS *Cole* and the French oil tanker MV *Limburg*, Yemen experienced a brief period of calm. Analysts now believe this was the result of a short-lived "tacit non-aggression pact" between the government and extremists and of enhanced U.S.–Yemeni counterterrorism cooperation. Several years later, however, a generational split by younger extremists, radicalized in part by the global Sunni Islamist revival and the U.S.-led invasion of Iraq, led to the emergence of a group not interested in negotiating with what it viewed as an illegitimate and un-Islamic government. Several prison escapes of experienced and dangerous operatives further energized this younger faction, which launched a new campaign of violent attacks against oil facilities, foreign residents and tourists, and government security targets. In September 2006, there were two near-simultaneous car bombings at oil facilities. Attacks against energy targets, including bombings of oil pipelines and shootings of oil field workers, have since occurred at a steady pace. (Not all attacks have been carried out by al-Qaeda, and determining responsibility for some attacks in Yemen is difficult. See the appendix at the end of this chapter for a listing of recent attacks.) Tourists have been killed in bombings and shootings in Marib in 2007 and in Hadramaut in 2008 and 2009. Starting in March 2008, violence moved to the capital, with a series of mortar and indirect fire attacks on the U.S. Embassy, Yemeni government facilities, and a Western housing compound. The offices of a Canadian oil company were bombed, and the U.S. Embassy was attacked again in September 2008 by multiple car bombs and gunmen.

There are increasing indications that al-Qaeda is regrouping in Yemen and preparing to strike at Western and other targets. Recent counterterrorism measures in Saudi Arabia have forced extremists to seek refuge elsewhere, and analysts have observed a steady flow relocating to Yemen's under-governed areas. In spring 2008, al-Qaeda operatives in Saudi Arabia were encouraged by local Saudi commanders to escape to Yemen, and by January 2009, the Saudi and Yemeni al-Qaeda affiliates merged. A video announcing the establishment of al-Qaeda in the Arabian Peninsula featured two Saudis who had been released from the U.S. military detention center at Guantanamo Bay, Cuba, and had assumed leadership positions in the newly formed organization. Following this news, Saudi authorities released a list of 85 most-wanted terrorism suspects. Of them, 26 were believed to be in Yemen, including a total of eleven Saudis who had been detained at Guantanamo.[5]

The emergence of the regional al-Qaeda group marks a major deterioration of security in Yemen. It is feared that Yemen may now be used by al-Qaeda as a base in the Arabian Peninsula to stage attacks in the Gulf and Horn of Africa. For the past several years, there have been reports of Saudi nationals killed or captured by security forces in Yemen. In April 2009, Saudi authorities announced the capture of eleven fighters who had crossed into Saudi Arabia from Yemen. The group allegedly possessed components for more than 30 suicide vests. This was the first concrete indication of Yemeni instability threatening Saudi security.

Dennis Blair, the U.S. director of national intelligence, highlighted the threat of a resurgent al-Qaeda organization in Yemen in testimony before the U.S. Senate Select Committee on Intelligence in February 2009. In his annual threat assessment, Blair noted that Yemen was "reemerging as a jihadist battleground and potential regional base of operations for al-Qaeda to plan internal and external attacks, train terrorists, and facilitate the movement of operatives." General David Petraeus, commander of the U.S. Central Command, echoed this warning in April 2009. Speaking before the House Armed Services Committee, he warned that "Yemen stands out from its neighbors on the Peninsula. The inability of the Yemeni government to secure and exercise control over all of its territory offers terrorist and insurgent groups in the region, particularly al-Qaeda, a safe haven in which to plan, organize, and support terrorist operations." Al-Qaeda's resurgence in Yemen is increasingly becoming a reality.

Yet by most accounts, it appears that terrorism directed or inspired by al-Qaeda is not a first order of concern for the Yemeni government. For the central government, the civil war in Saada and the secessionist movement in the South represent threats to the very survival of the state. There is no disputing that the Yemeni government and its interests have been targeted by al-Qaeda, and in discussions with foreigners, senior Yemeni officials often note that their country is combating terrorism. But U.S. officials express exasperation at Yemen's seemingly on-again, off-again cooperation on counterterrorism issues. Washington has been particularly frustrated by the perception that accused terrorists in Yemen benefit from a government policy of "catch and release" because a number of high-profile suspects have either been released from custody or have escaped from detention in Yemen, at times allegedly with the help of the security services. The U.S. government is also seeking to extradite two Yemeni nationals on charges of terrorism—Jamal al-Badawi, charged with involvement in the attack on the USS *Cole*, and Jaber Elbaneh, wanted in connection with the so-called Lackawanna Six case, a group of Yemeni-Americans who went to an al-Qaeda camp in Afghanistan in 2001. In part because of a constitutional prohibition on extradition, Yemeni authorities have not turned over either suspect to the United States despite repeated requests. Two prison escapes of suspected al-Qaeda members—ten from Aden in 2003 and 23 from Sanaa in 2006—led many observers to decry the inability of the Yemeni government to keep terror suspects behind bars.

WAR IN SAADA. Since 2004, the Yemeni government has been fighting a sporadic civil war against Zaidi Shi'i revivalists in the northern province of Saada. The conflict followed anti-government demonstrations by members of the Believing Youth movement. Militants disrupted mosque services in Saada, shouting anti-government, anti-American, and anti-Israeli slogans. The disturbances spread to Sanaa, with protesters criticizing the Saleh regime for its counterterrorism cooperation with the United States. After an unsuccessful reconciliation effort, the government attempted to arrest Zaidi leader Hussein Badreddine al-Houthi, a former member of parliament. The government accused him of fomenting unrest and seeking to revive the Zaidi imamate that had been overthrown in the 1962 republican revolution. The conflict quickly escalated, and although al-Houthi was killed in September 2004, fighting has continued under the leadership of the al-Houthi family.

Sanaa claims that the rebels seek to overthrow the current government and establish a theocracy. Throughout the conflict, the Yemeni government has sought to link the rebellion to the larger "war on terrorism" and has accused the Iranian government of supporting the Shi'i guerrillas. To date, there is no public evidence to support the allegations of Iranian meddling. The origins of the conflict are in fact a complex combination of competing sectarian identities, regional underdevelopment, perceived socioeconomic injustices, and historical grievances.[6] The conflict is exacerbated by tensions between the indigenous Zaidi Shi'i population and Sunni Salafi fundamentalists who have relocated to the area. Moreover, it has taken on a tribal hue after the regime sought to recruit tribal fighters to combat the insurrection.

By spring 2009, there were five separate rounds of fighting in Saada. The Qatari government in 2007 unsuccessfully attempted to mediate a lasting cease-fire. Over the course of the conflict, fighting has been at times both fierce and indiscriminate, punctuated by periods of relative calm brought about in part when government forces have exhausted munitions. By 2008, fighting had spread outside Saada into other governorates and to the outskirts of Sanaa, leading President Saleh to declare a unilateral cease-fire in July 2008 on the thirtieth anniversary of his rule. The toll has been severe in Saada, including extensive damage to infrastructure, an estimated 130,000 internally displaced people, and extremely limited humanitarian relief and reconstruction efforts. These factors continue to exacerbate matters, leaving tensions high and further fighting likely.

Over the course of the five-year conflict, much of the Yemeni army has seen combat in Saada. The strain has led to questions about the military's ability to simultaneously engage in other operations such as combating Islamist extremism. Moreover, the inability of the government to decisively put down the rebellion has prompted concerns that other domestic challengers may be emboldened and perceive the regime as vulnerable. Islamist militants or other disaffected groups could mount attacks on other fronts while the government is distracted by the war in Saada.

SOUTHERN SECESSIONIST MOVEMENT.   A third major security concern is the mounting southern secessionist movement. Since unification, the former South Yemen has complained of economic and social marginalization by the northern-led government. This has recently led to renewed protests and increasing fears that the South may seek independence. Central to southern disaffection are economic grievances, both real and perceived. Oil—Yemen's primary source of income—is located mostly in the South, yet the region has seen little economic development. While conditions are not much better in the North, there is a popular perception by southerners that their region has been excluded from its fair share of oil revenue. Moreover, southern tribal networks never fully re-emerged after being suppressed by the government of the People's Democratic Republic of Yemen prior to unification in 1990. The importation of different northern tribal structures and patronage networks has further inflamed southern separatist feelings.

The southern issue resurfaced in September 2007 following protests by former southern military officers demanding reinstated pensions, along with renewed feelings of political disenfranchisement and exclusion from government jobs and services. Southern leaders have asserted that the North has not followed through on commitments to improve conditions made after unification and the civil war in 1994. Tensions, protests, and sporadic violence followed. What began with demands for reform gradually turned to calls for southern independence. In response, the government has increasingly used greater levels of repression—security crackdowns, arrests, episodes of periodic violence, and closure of several southern newspapers—in an attempt to contain the separatist aspirations. The government has announced plans to try separatist agitators and to create a new court to try members of the press involved in publishing material considered "damaging to national unity."

Like the war in Saada, conditions in the South pose an existential threat to the Republic of Yemen but with a greater and broader appeal. Moreover, it is an extremely delicate issue and one that recalls previous crises, including unification and the civil war. The potential scope of the separatist challenge to the Saleh regime was made evident in spring 2009 when an important regime supporter defected to the southern movement. Tariq al-Fadhli, a former *mujahid* who had fought in Afghanistan, has family roots in the South including claims to hereditary lands. According to some analyses, the withdrawal of al-Fadhli's support for the government is symptomatic of the southern issue's propensity to challenge the status quo.

PIRACY AND BORDER SECURITY. Yemen has been unable to secure its borders, and as a result it has become a key transit point for guns, drugs, and other smuggling, from East Africa through Saudi Arabia to the Gulf states. Saudi border guards note the large quantities of drugs seized at the border with Yemen, in addition to the continual influx of illegal laborers. Weapons from Yemen have allegedly been used in attacks within Saudi Arabia, including explosives employed in a Riyadh bombing and assault rifles used in the attack on the U.S. consulate in Jiddah.

The recent surge in piracy has also had a major impact on Yemen. In the first six months of this year, 130 piracy incidents occurred in the Gulf of Aden and off the coast of Somalia, compared with 111 attacks in all of 2008. According to Yemeni government figures released in July 2009, piracy in the Gulf of Aden has cost the country an estimated $150 million in security expenses and increased insurance premiums and roughly $200 million in lost fishing and other revenue.

Addressing the Convergence of Problems

The interlocking challenges outlined in this paper have the potential to overwhelm the Yemeni government. At the heart of the problem is the central government's failure to exercise full control and authority throughout the entire national territory. A critical paradox is that expanding the presence of the government throughout the country potentially means delegitimizing the government, because expanding state control has long been synonymous with imposing northern, Sanaan control. This also touches on sensitive issues related to tribal identity. Much of the population outside major highland urban areas associates the Saleh regime with corruption, cronyism, nepotism, and blocked economic and social opportunities; therefore, expanding central government control risks alienating more of the population. This inverse relationship between levels of central government control and regional resistance and resentment has historically frustrated governance efforts in Yemen.

The Yemeni government and major international donors have sought to address Yemen's rapidly converging problems, with varying degrees of success. Sanaa has outlined an ambitious yet vague approach centered on strengthening the government's control through decentralization. Major donors have increased financial assistance and implemented programs designed to reduce the impact of Yemen's problems, although more needs to be done. Ultimately, the interconnected problems facing Yemen will require domestic, regional, and international coordination to resolve.

The Government of Yemen's Efforts to Date

Despite facing severe financial limitations, the Yemeni government has identified several broad focus areas, including efforts to boost the economy and to expand government control. For instance, the Ministry of Planning and International Cooperation wants to increase the Social Welfare Fund and expand the number of beneficiaries of government assistance. The planning minister, Abdulkarim al-Arhabi, also advocates incentivizing government assistance programs by offering temporary assistance based in part on certain conditions, such as keeping children in school or successfully completing adult skill training courses.

While addressing the economy merits urgent attention, little is known about how the government plans to go about this. Broad goals have been set, although it is not clear how any of them would be implemented. According to several senior officials, Yemen's strategic plans for dealing with the economy are made up of seven interconnected goals: integrating Yemen in the Gulf Cooperation Council; encouraging oil and gas exploration; promoting non-hydrocarbon foreign investment; increasing aid and development assistance; reforming the business environment; addressing population growth; and expanding education opportunities. These ambitious objectives seek to address many of the issues discussed in this chapter, although specific measures to advance these goals have not yet been enumerated.

In the near term, the Yemeni government will need to address the economic status quo, the rise of under-governed spaces, and the looming water crisis.

A POST-OIL ECONOMY? Yemeni officials have done little serious planning to prepare for a viable post-oil economy. Options being discussed include mineral exploitation, tourism, and maritime shipping and trade services. The mining of gold, silver, zinc, granite, and marble are under consideration by the Ministry of Oil and Minerals as potential projects, although infrastructure concerns have been noted about all such mining. The Economist Intelligence Unit reports that a major zinc project began in February 2009, with exports scheduled for 2010. It estimates that the twelve-year project will contribute $600 million to the national economy and employ more than 350 Yemeni nationals. Commercial fishing also has potential, although according to senior Yemeni officials, marine resources would require judicious management to prevent over-fishing and depletion.

Senior officials have also proposed tourism, noting Yemen's rich cultural heritage. Such plans would be subject to security considerations, because several recent incidents of terrorist attacks have been directed against foreign tourists visiting historical sites. Eight Spaniards were killed in a July 2007 bombing at Bilqis Temple in Marib, and two Belgians and four South Koreans were killed in separate attacks in Hadramaut in January 2008 and March 2009, respectively.

With more than 2,200 kilometers, or 1,367 miles, of coastline alongside one of the world's busiest shipping lanes, on paper Yemen would seem to be perfectly positioned to offer shipping and related services. The port of Aden is one of the world's greatest natural deepwater harbors and currently includes a container terminal, oil harbor, and other facilities. Originally used as a coaling station for the British Royal Navy, it could potentially service commercial and other traffic. Plans to develop the port suffered a major setback following an attack on the USS *Cole* during a refueling stop in October 2000 that killed seventeen U.S. sailors. (An attempted attack a few months earlier against another American warship refueling at Aden, USS *The Sullivans*, failed when the small boat carrying the explosives sank under its own weight.) Security concerns were again highlighted after the October 2002 attack on the MV *Limburg* that killed one crew member and spilled 90,000 barrels of oil. After the *Limburg* attack, insurance premiums for ships using the Port of Aden soared, traffic dropped off, and the foreign operator, Port of Singapore Authority, ended its contract. It has been suggested recently that Aden could host cruise ships, but security concerns and exorbitant insurance premiums make this an extremely unlikely prospect.

The most promising source of near-term potential revenue appears to be sales of liquefied natural gas. An ambitious and large-scale natural gas liquefaction project has been under way in Yemen since the mid-1990s. After numerous false starts and other obstacles, it was scheduled to begin operation in mid-2009. Experts have raised several concerns about the Total S.A.–led project, ranging from human capacity and technical issues to doubts about physical infrastructure security and market viability. According to a report by the World Bank, the government of Yemen would earn about $10.8 billion in royalties, bonuses, and taxes from the project over a twenty-year period through 2028.[7] Several billion dollars in other income from dividends and operating fees are also likely during that period. To be sure, this is revenue that Sanaa badly needs. But even in a best-case scenario, income from exports of liquefied natural gas would only offset the drop in revenue from oil exports and not replace oil income. This is because, among other reasons, global liquefied natural gas prices have dropped and there are no guaranteed customers. Furthermore, it is very likely that the Yemeni government will experience a period of curtailed revenue between the end of oil exports and the onset of new income from the sale of liquefied natural gas, during which Yemen's other crises will worsen. In the end, even Yemen's natural gas reserves are limited, and they, too, will eventually run out. Revenue derived from liquefied natural gas thus will only postpone the inevitable — shifting to a post-hydrocarbon economy.

PLANNED DECENTRALIZATION.   One potentially critical policy being developed by the Yemeni government is to transfer control from the central government to regional governorates. This decentralization strategy seeks to recognize the de facto autonomy that exists in several areas of the country. By granting more responsibility to such areas, Sanaa asserts that local governments will in turn perform more professionally. This is a gradual and ongoing process, and Yemeni officials have noted that not all governorates are up to the task. According to officials, large national functions such as enacting legislation and setting and monitoring strategic goals would be retained by the central government, while localities would be responsible for building roads, schools, and health care centers. This is to be financed through a combination of local resources, such as unspecified fees collected by local authorities and central resources that the regime would distribute to local authorities.

In essence, this strategy institutionalizes the informal patronage systems that have served in lieu of durable national governance bodies, and it encourages the further development of regionalism at the expense of the central government. It is also a tacit recognition that outlying regions operate outside of central government control. Government officials argue that the capital will be able to manage the governorate through such tools as the ruling General People's Congress party apparatus, thereby enabling Sanaa a say in who leads local governorates. The state also plans to use the party apparatus to combat what it has identified as the biggest challenges to decentralization: poverty, illiteracy, and tribalism.

Ultimately, it appears that such a policy would involve the central government's selecting a local leader who would then be granted limited autonomy in exchange for certain levels of governance and provisions of social services. This is to be controlled through local council elections and the eventual elections of regional governors, in processes largely guided by the ruling party.

Official government-directed decentralization merely grants the state's imprimatur on the status quo throughout much of the country. It is unclear how localities would fund social services when the central government is unable to do so now. Given that the primary objective vis-à-vis state stability in Yemen is to instill some control over what are now under-governed territories and to prevent the emergence of other under-governed territories, officially limiting the central government's role is counterproductive at best. Building robust institutions able to deliver social services and safeguard local populations is essential.

THE PENDING WATER CRISIS. The rapidly decreasing availability of water also demands immediate attention. The urgency of the pending crisis is obscured by the fact that water resource depletion is a gradual process that will occur throughout the country at different times. The immediate onset of Yemen's water crisis may therefore go unnoticed by the regime and by international policy makers as outlying regions and governorates experience chronic shortages and high prices for water before other, more central, urban areas.

Despite government recognition of the problem, the issue is not a priority for Sanaa. Al-Iryani, the water and environment minister, has observed that until the state elevates water conservation to be a national concern—as was done in 2007 to ban weapons in Sanaa—little movement will be made. Addressing the issue of water will require broad coordination among ministries, as well as tackling a number of sensitive subjects such as corruption, government priorities, budgetary subsidies, and societal norms.

There are no easy solutions. Other Gulf states have resorted to the desalinization of seawater; that is unfeasible in Yemen, however, because fuel costs are so high (Yemen's hydrocarbon reserves are far more modest than elsewhere and are already slated for export) and because the desalinated water would have to be pumped up more than 7,000 feet to reach the capital and other major population centers in the highlands.

More feasible for Yemen would be the reintroduction and modernization of traditional methods of agriculture and irrigation. Curbing government subsidies and purchases of qat for official functions could also be effective. Encouraging the importation of qat from East Africa and helping farmers transition to growing cereals and foodstuffs would also help curtail water usage, though admittedly that would prove difficult because growing qat is far more profitable for farmers. Enacting a legal regime to govern the use and distribution of groundwater is also an imperative. If such measures are not taken in the near term, more dramatic steps will be required in the future, such as stopping rural populations from moving to overcrowded cities, and, more drastically, relocating population centers from the center of the country to the coasts.

The Efforts of Major Donors

Since the 1970s, Yemen has been dependent upon foreign aid. According to Yemeni government officials, the country receives on average $13 to $15 per capita in total foreign aid money—less per capita, they point out, than many sub-Saharan Africa countries receive. While the veracity of these figures may be in doubt, they demonstrate the perception among senior Yemeni officials that their country receives inadequate international attention, considering Yemen's critical strategic importance and the risks to regional stability and security that are associated with the many problems facing the country.

In apparent recognition of Yemen's challenges, the United Kingdom recently increased its aid to the country by 400 percent. Its Department for International Development's commitment of £50 million (or $83 million) per year for the next five years makes the UK the single largest foreign donor in Yemen.[8]

Several other European nations run modest development assistance projects in Yemen focusing on reproductive health issues, acute maternal care, obstetric education and training, and small-scale family planning projects. Rural education programs administered by Yemen's Social Fund for Development have also received funding, as have water management programs. By comparison, Arab countries and Islamic funds have contributed significantly more total funds in both grants and smaller loans. Saudi Arabia has been one of the largest total donors, providing investment, grants, and nearly annual direct budgetary support. According to Ministry of Planning and International Cooperation officials and others, European donors tend to support soft projects, while Arab donors more often support capital infrastructure development.

Yemen critically needs assistance in making sure that projects receive ongoing funding. For example, from a public health standpoint, the country needs greater education, training, basic medical supplies, and continued support for existing projects. In the future, Yemen will need to better coordinate international donors to maximize the impact of foreign assistance.

Total U.S. aid for Yemen in fiscal 2009 is $27.5 million, of which $21 million is development assistance. The remainder includes Foreign Military Financing, counterterrorism and related programs, and International Military and Education Training.[9] Although the total aid package is about $7 million more than in fiscal 2008, it is disproportionately small considering the strategic importance of Yemen to U.S. foreign policy and national security interests and the magnitude of the problems facing Yemen. By comparison, in fiscal 2008 Pakistan received an estimated $1.8 billion in combined security and economic assistance. This disparity exists even as U.S. officials increasingly cite Yemen as a terrorism and security priority second only to Afghanistan and Pakistan. The Obama administration has requested that U.S. aid to Yemen more than double for fiscal 2010 to more than $50 million, excluding military and security funding. U.S. military and security funding for fiscal 2010 will jump to more than $66 million for counterterrorism, anti-piracy, and border security assistance—more than double the amount for the two previous years combined.

Foreign assistance to Yemen is hampered by concerns related to domestic corruption and capacity limitations. A major question for foreign donors is whether Yemen has the capacity at present to absorb more aid money. There is consensus that Yemen desperately needs more financial assistance to address stability concerns and to help provide public services. These concerns are compounded by perceptions that Yemen lacks educated professionals to run more programs. The deteriorating security conditions complicate matters; the inability to guarantee the safety of Westerners working on development projects is a significant concern.

Ways to Help

It is essential that Washington take a holistic approach to Yemen. Although the major U.S. foreign policy concern with regard to Yemen since 2001 has been security and counterterrorism, the country's deteriorating security is a result of problems unrelated to security. As such, in many cases development assistance, education and technical cooperation, capacity building, institution strengthening, and direct financial assistance can better address the interconnected challenges facing Yemen than can military and security aid.

Framing the U.S.–Yemeni relationship as based solely on security and counterterrorism issues, to the near exclusion of all other issues, has meant that movement on all other issues has been subject to Washington's perception of progress and cooperation from Sanaa on counterterrorism issues. As a result, a lack of movement on counterterrorism issues has stalled all other interactions (and the fact that Yemen is slated to receive more U.S. military and security assistance funding than development assistance in fiscal 2010 demonstrates a continued misallocation of priorities). The United States has ongoing foreign policy and national security interests with regard to Yemen that extend beyond counterterrorism issues, and so it is in Washington's interests to engage Yemen on other issues that will contribute indirectly to improving domestic security.

Yemen should be viewed as part of the Horn of Africa *and* the Arabian Peninsula. While geographically part of the Arabian Peninsula, Yemen in fact has little else in common with the Gulf Cooperation Council states. To be sure, there are many deep connections between Yemeni and Saudi society, but the income disparity and differences in public service provision between Yemen and the Gulf Cooperation Council states clearly point to their differing problems, challenges, and capabilities. In many respects,

Yemen's problems more closely approximate those of neighboring East Africa. Yemen's deep ties with the Horn of Africa and role in a greater East Africa smuggling and security complex further underscore the need to view Yemen with a broader lens.

Looking forward, there will be a greater need to improve donor coordination and assistance programs—all the more so because the ongoing global financial crisis will further strain international assistance programs. The Yemeni government currently does a poor job of managing international assistance, and international donors need better synchronization to maximize their impact.

Increased financial assistance to Yemen, such as that currently proposed for fiscal 2010, is required. Assistance can be used to support and offset the difficult economic choices that will need to be made in Yemen, such as curbing government subsidies on diesel and introducing agricultural diversification. Local capacity-building efforts, such as English language instruction, teacher training courses, micro-finance enterprises, and exchange programs for judges, members of parliament, journalists, government workers, and academics can help fill voids left by reduced state capacity.

On security issues, strengthening border guard units so that the central government can better secure its own national borders is a first-order priority. This must be done in coordination with other regional neighbors including Saudi Arabia and Oman. Since 2001, the United States has taken steps toward this objective by supporting the establishment of the Yemeni coast guard and conducting needs assessments of the border guard units. However, senior Yemeni officers report that there has been little follow-through, and both the coast guard and border guards are in desperate need of equipment and training—something the bulk of U.S. security assistance for fiscal 2010 is intended to provide. Increased military-to-military training and exchanges with both the United States and other regional partners should also take place.

Yemen's ability to combat terrorism must be bolstered through efforts to build local capacity in law enforcement and in the legal and judicial systems. Enacting counterterrorism legislation and terror finance laws would help build state resilience. Greater policing training and programs to professionalize the prison service can help staunch one of the greatest concerns held by Western counterterrorism officials. In areas where it is not feasible or desirable to partner with the United States, such efforts can utilize the unique assets of European nations and other regional states.

Ultimately, a regional approach is needed to help improve stability in Yemen. The threats posed to Yemeni security and stability will jeopardize interests well beyond Yemen's borders, and as such there is not solely a U.S., European, or regional solution to Yemen's many challenges. The only way to mitigate the impact of these problems is through the active involvement of all stakeholders. Saudi Arabia and other Gulf Cooperation Council states need to be encouraged to take greater action because failure to address Yemen's looming challenges would hit the regional states first and hardest. Washington should encourage the Gulf states to hold out membership in the Gulf Cooperation Council for Yemen in exchange for tough steps, including progress on curbing government subsidies, addressing corruption, and enacting measures to curtail security concerns. The council should also open trade with Yemen and formalize labor movements to help create a viable and durable future for the country. Yemen should establish high coordination commissions (like the one that exists with Saudi Arabia) with other Gulf states. The international community will also need to help mediate the southern secessionist issue, support a cease-fire in Saada, and begin reconstruction and development assistance to these regions.

Conclusion

Senior Yemeni officials have acknowledged that the country's economic challenges complicate and worsen its security concerns. Development plans, poverty limitation efforts, employment schemes, and public service provision have all been adversely affected by the linkages between the economy and security. Furthermore, domestic unrest and Islamist terrorism have done much to damage the reputation of Yemen as a foreign investment location.

The challenges and problems facing Yemen are not unique in the region. Throughout the Middle East, an increasing number of countries face similar problems of deteriorating state capacity and rising economic and demographic instability. However, in Yemen these challenges threaten to disrupt not just local stability, but also regional and international stability, including the flow of vital hydrocarbons. If left unaddressed, Yemen's problems could potentially destabilize Saudi Arabia and the other Gulf states. The inability of the Yemeni central government to fully control its territory will create space for violent extremists to regroup and launch attacks against domestic and international targets. The international community must be realistic about the limitations of intervention in Yemen. In the near term, however, inaction is not an option.

Notes

1. Eurasia Group, "Yemen Outlook," December 9, 2008, p. 3.

2. Ginny Hill, "Yemen: Fear of Failure," Chatham House briefing paper, November 2008, p. 10.

3. World Bank, "Yemen: Towards Qat Demand Reduction," Report No. 39738-YE, June 2007, http://www-wds.worldbank.org/external/default/WDSContentServer/WDSP/IB/2007/06/26/000090341_20070626112355/Rendered/PDF/397380YE.pdf, p. 2.

4. Bernard Haykel, "Rebellion, Migration or Consultative Democracy? The Zaidis and their Detractors in Yemen," in R. Leveau, F. Mermier, and U. Steinbach, eds., *Le Yémen Contemporain* (Paris: Karthala, 1999), p. 196.

5. One of the Guantanamo returnees featured in the video, Muhammad al-Awfi, was repatriated to Saudi Arabia in mid-February 2009. Two other of the 85 most-wanted suspects are believed to have been apprehended in Yemen.

6. See recent International Crisis Group report, "Yemen: Defusing the Saada Time Bomb," May 27, 2009, for a comprehensive overview of the conflict.

7. World Bank, "Republic of Yemen: A Natural Gas Incentive Framework," June 2007, p. 5.

8. Department for International Development, "Yemen: Our Current Program," 2008.

9. Jeremy Sharp, "Yemen: Background and U.S. Relations," Congressional Research Service Report, January 2009, p. 15.

Appendix: Timeline of Recent Attacks

December 1992	Bombing of 2 Aden hotels billeting U.S. troops en route to Somalia for Operation Restore Hope
December 1992	Militants arrested for targeting American aircraft at Aden airport
December 1998	Militants associated with the Islamic Army of Aden–Abyan (IAAA) detained for planning attacks against British Embassy and other targets
December 1998	16 Western tourists kidnapped by IAAA; four tourists fatally shot during gunfight with government forces
October 1999	IAAA founder Zain al-Abidan abu Bakr al-Midhar hanged
January 2000	Failed attack against USS *The Sullivans* in Aden harbor
October 2000	USS *Cole* attack in Aden harbor kills 17 sailors
October 2000	Explosion at UK Embassy in Sanaa
April 2002	Small explosion near U.S. Embassy in Sanaa
October 2002	French oil tanker MV *Limburg* bombed
November 2002	Abu Ali al-Harithi, a senior al-Qaeda leader linked to attacks on the USS *Cole* and the *Limburg*, killed in U.S. Predator attack
November 2002	Shots fired at Hunt Oil Company helicopter in Sanaa
December 2002	3 U.S. missionary doctors killed in Jibla
March 2003	Marib oil field shooting
April 2003	10 prisoners, including several alleged USS *Cole* bombers, escape from Aden prison
December 2003	Yemeni security official assassinated
February 2006	23 prisoners, including suspected al-Qaeda members, escape from Sanaa prison
September 2006	Synchronized car bombings of oil facilities in Marib and Mukalla
October 2006	Aden pipeline bombing
February 2007	Shootout foils attempted pipeline bombing

March 2007	Assassination of chief investigator in Marib
June 2007	Shabwa oil field shooting
July 2007	Bombing at Bilqis Temple in Marib kills 8 Spanish tourists and 2 Yemenis
August 2007	Attack on power station and government building in Marib
November 2007	Pipeline bombing southeast of Sanaa
December 2007	Pipeline bombing southeast of Sanaa
December 2007	Bombing of 2 security locations in Hadramaut
January 2008	Fatal shooting of 2 Belgian tourists and 2 Yemenis in Hadramaut
March 2008	2 bombings in Abyan
March 2008	Mortar attack near U.S. Embassy in Sanaa
March 2008	Alleged mortar attack on Chinese oil facility in Hadramaut
March 2008	Bombing in Aden
March 2008	Bombing of oil pipeline
April 2008	Mortar attack on Western housing compound in Sanaa
April 2008	Bombing at Canadian Nexen oil company office in Sanaa
April 2008	Bombing at security facility in Sayyoun
April 2008	Mortar attack on Italian Embassy and Yemeni Customs Authority
April 2008	Japanese tanker *Takayama* hit by rocket-propelled grenade (pirates suspected)
May 2008	Bombing at Saada mosque kills 15
May 2008	Mortar allegedly fired at presidential palace in Sanaa
June 2008	Failed rocket attack on Aden refinery
July 2008	Suicide bombing of police station in Sayyoun
August 2008	Mortar attack in Mukalla
September 2008	Attack on U.S. Embassy in Sanaa kills 16, including 6 attackers

Timeline (continued)

January 2009	Release of video announcing merger of Saudi and Yemeni al-Qaeda affiliates
February 2009	4 South Korean tourists and Yemeni guide killed in suicide bombing in Shibam; subsequent suicide bombing targets motorcade in Sanaa carrying victims' relatives
June 2009	Kidnapping of 9 foreign aid workers in Saada, 3 of whom appear to have been executed after their abduction
July 2009	Pipeline operated by South Korean firm bombed in Shabwa
July 2009	Pipeline attack east of Sanaa thwarted

EXPLOITING GRIEVANCES: AL-QAEDA IN THE ARABIAN PENINSULA

Alistair Harris

There is a consensus that Yemeni, regional, and international security is threatened by AQAP. In a recent (February 2010) edition of AQAP's bimonthly e-magazine *Sada al-Malahim* (The Echo of Epic Battles), an author using the nom de plume Hamil al-Misk (The Musk Bearer) emphasized that the organization had now moved from a defensive to an offensive mode of operation:

> We bring to our nation the good news that the mujahideen passed the stage of defense and repulsion of the aggression to the stage where they can take initiatives and attack.[1]

Following the attempted assassination of Saudi Assistant Minister of Interior for Security Affairs Prince Muhammad bin Nayef bin Abdulaziz in August 2009[2] and the failed attempt by 23-year-old Nigerian Umar Farouk Abdulmutallab to detonate an explosive device on a flight to Detroit on Christmas Day last year,[3] the U.S. response was swift and predictable. CENTCOM Commander General David Petraeus immediately visited Yemen and announced the American intention to double security aid to the country.[4] In the face of increasingly alarmist claims about the nature of the threat posed by AQAP, U.S.-assisted missile and air strikes have attempted to decapitate AQAP in a series of targeted strikes.[5] Such a strategy had proved effective in 2002, when an American drone killed the head of al-Qaeda in Yemen at the time, Abu Ali al-Harithi.

Dealing with symptoms is no substitute for dealing with causes, however. In the rush to offer prescriptive advice, key questions remain unanswered.

What do we actually know about AQAP? How has the organization evolved in terms of membership, structure, tactics, and goals? What is it trying to achieve, and crucially, why? What lessons can we learn for countering processes of radicalization? Prevention and the promotion of community resilience, as much as protective and offensive measures, need to form part of the counterterrorism tool kit.

The Evolution of al-Qaeda in the Arabian Peninsula

In a statement released on February 8, 2010, AQAP's deputy leader Saeed al-Shihri gave a clear indication of the nature of the relationship of the organization to what is termed "al-Qaeda core," the nucleus of al-Qaeda operating in the border area between Afghanistan and Pakistan. Al-Shihri addressed his comments to "our sheikhs and amirs in the general command in Khorasan [Afghanistan]" and in doing so described those self-identified as al-Qaeda in the Arabian Peninsula as "your mujahideen children in the Peninsula of Mohammad."[6] The raised profile of the current incarnation of the organization should not detract from an awareness of al-Qaeda's enduring presence in Yemen.

Particularly since this near miss on December 25, 2009, it has been tempting to analyze AQAP as a new, little-known threat. In reality, much information is available about the organization. Because AQAP is the product of the fusion of al-Qaeda's Saudi and Yemeni branches, much can be learned from the successes and failures of both al-Qaeda in Saudi Arabia and the counterterrorist response. Equally illuminating is the study of the media output of al-Qaeda's franchise in Saudi Arabia, from the tactical and military publication *Mu'askar al-Battar* (al-Battar Training Camp) to its sister political publication *Sawt al-Jihad* (Voice of Jihad) and specific treatises, such as the seminal "A Practical Course for Guerilla Warfare," by former al-Qaeda leader in Saudi Arabia, Abdel Aziz Issa Abdul-Mohsin al-Muqrin. As we seek to draw conclusions about the organizational nature and threat posed by AQAP, taking time to analyze the tactical, operational, strategic, and ideational precursors for the group pays dividends. As Norman Cigar argues, "Access to al-Qaeda's doctrinal literature can provide valuable insights into the latter organization's planning, training, and operational thinking—insights that can help policy makers shape a more realistic profile of its leaders and of its strategy, which can be key in developing effective counterterrorism and counterinsurgency policies."[7]

Sada al-Malahim and Frameworks of Collective Action

Considered alongside its attack record, a detailed analysis of AQAP's media output provides telling insights into the group. Such output shows how al-Qaeda tries to make different ideas, beliefs, myths, and traditions work to radicalize and mobilize the population. Al-Qaeda's publications provide a diagnosis of the problems faced by Yemenis, detailing grievances and apportioning blame. It also provides a prognosis for the future, proposing remedies and redress. In other words, AQAP provides both diagnostic and prognostic frameworks to mobilize followers and potential recruits into collective action.[8] AQAP's success as an organization depends entirely on the extent to which its frames resonate with the Yemeni population. In the face of debilitating law enforcement activity, AQAP faces the problem of constantly regenerating by recruiting new members; if it fails, it will pass into obscurity. Whether AQAP will endure and present an increasing security threat therefore depends on the extent to which its message resonates with local communities.

Even a cursory examination of *Sada al-Malahim* indicates that AQAP's diagnostic framework is designed to have a broad appeal and is likely to resonate successfully in Yemen. This has led seasoned analyst Gregory Johnsen to state in a recent Senate hearing that "al-Qaeda is the most representative organization in Yemen. It transcends class, tribe, and regional identity in a way that no other organization or political party does."[9] As evidence of this broad appeal, Murad Batal al-Shishani, based on a rudimentary analysis of known members of the organization, claims that Yemenis make up 56 percent of the AQAP's total membership, Saudis 37 percent, and foreigners 7 percent. According to al-Shishani, the Yemeni members are equally distributed between northern and southern tribes.[10] A shared grievance narrative has led to claims by Yemeni analysts that while al-Qaeda may number in the hundreds, there are tens of thousands of Yemenis who share their grievances.[11]

But a shared grievance does not imply agreement on means of redress, and it is this dissonance that holds the key to counterterrorism policy making in Yemen. Before considering the promotion of narrative dissonance as a counterterrorism tool, note that an analysis of *Sada al-Malahim* shows how AQAP has become increasingly successful in aligning its societal diagnosis with Yemeni grievances.

Timeline

December 29, 1992	Al-Qaeda targets the Gold Mohur hotel in the port of Aden, where U.S. military personnel are staying en route to Somalia. One Australian tourist is killed.
January 3, 2000	Al-Qaeda attempts a suicide attack on the USS *The Sullivans* in the port of Aden, but the attack craft sinks due to overloading.
October 12, 2000	The USS *Cole* is the object of an al-Qaeda maritime suicide attack in Aden. Seventeen U.S. naval personnel are killed and 39 are injured.
October 6, 2002	The French tanker *The Limburg* is the object of a maritime suicide attack in the Gulf of Aden. One Belgian crew member is killed and twelve others are injured.
November 3, 2002	The al-Qaeda leader in Yemen, Abu Ali al-Harithi, is killed by a U.S. Predator drone strike.
November 25, 2003	The Yemeni government arrests al-Harithi's replacement, Muhammad Hamdi al-Ahdal.
2003–2006	Al-Qaeda focuses on its confrontation with Saudi Arabia and is highly active inside the Kingdom. Yemenis are channeled toward participation in confrontations with coalition forces in Iraq.
February 3, 2006	A key moment in the emergence of a new al-Qaeda organization in Yemen as 23 prisoners escape from prison in Sanaa. This group makes up the nucleus of the organization known today as al-Qaeda in the Arabian Peninsula.[1] As the group consolidates itself under the leadership of Osama Bin Laden's former secretary, Nasir Abdel Karim al-Wuhayshi (a.k.a. Abu Basir), his deputy Said Ali al-Shihri, and military commander Qasim al-Raimi, its attacks increase in sophistication and lethality. In addition, the success of the Saudi counterterrorism program up to 2006 ensured that the al-Qaeda threat was displaced to Yemen.[2] Initially targeting the extractive industries sector, Al-Qaeda in Yemen, as the organization was then known, proceeded to utilize suicide bombings to target tourists and Western interests.
September 15, 2006	Failed simultaneous suicide bombings on oil and gas facilities in Hadramaut and Marib.
March 29, 2007	Assassination of Ali Mahmoud Qasaylah, chief criminal investigator in Marib.
June 21, 2007	Nasir al-Wuhayshi (Abu Basir) declared leader of AQAP by deputy Qasim al-Raymi (Abu Hureira al-Sanaani).

July 3, 2007	Seven Spanish tourists and their two Yemeni guides are killed in a suicide car bombing in Marib.
January 18, 2008	Two Belgian tourists and two Yemenis are killed in an attack in Hadramaut.
March 18, 2008	Grenade attack on U.S. Embassy.
April 6, 2008	Attacks are made on two military checkpoints in Hadramaut and a foreigners' housing compound in Sanaa.
April 30, 2008	The Italian Embassy is attacked with mortars.
September 17, 2008	Al-Qaeda attacks the U.S. Embassy. At least 17 people killed.
January 2009	Saudi and Yemeni branches of al-Qaeda are merged into a regional franchise—Al-Qaeda in the Arabian Peninsula—which pledged allegiance to al-Qaeda. Targeting of key security personnel increased. An increasingly sophisticated use of the media and communications technology is apparent in the group's magazine, *Sada al-Malahim,* first distributed in 2008 and now in its twelfth edition. A focus on outreach is matched by a commitment to innovation, best evidenced by the use of a foreign student traveling from a European city to attempt to down a Detroit-bound plane with concealed explosives on Christmas Day in 2009.
March 15, 2009	A suicide bomber kills four South Korean tourists and their Yemeni guide. Three days later, a convoy of the victims' relatives and South Korean investigators is targeted in another suicide attack, but only the bomber is killed.
March 18, 2009	A suicide attack is attempted against a convoy of vehicles on the road to Sanaa International Airport.
August 28, 2009	An assassination is attempted against Saudi Assistant Minister of Interior for Security Affairs Prince Muhammad bin Nayef bin Abdulaziz.
December 25, 2009	Nigerian student Umar Farouk Abdulmutallab tries to detonate explosives in a plane over Detroit. AQAP claims responsibility for the attack.

1. Gregory D. Johnsen, "Tracking Yemen's 23 Escaped Jihadis—Part 1," *Terrorism Monitor,* vol. 5, January 18, 2007, p. 18; Gregory D. Johnsen, "Tracking Yemen's 23 Escaped Jihadis—Part 2," *Terrorism Monitor,* vol. 5, January 18, 2007, p. 19.

2. The arrest of 113 suspected Al-Qaeda members in Saudi Arabia announced on March 25, 2010, as well as the attempted infiltration of al-Qaeda operatives Yousuf Muhammad Mubarak al-Shihra and Raed Abdullah Salim al-Harbi into Saudi Arabia's Jazan province in October 2009 confirm that attacks inside the Saudi Kingdom remain a priority for Al-Qaeda in the Arabian Peninsula.

Identifying Grievances—AQAP's Diagnostic Framework

AQAP proffers a coherent grievance narrative that is consistent with the core tenets of al-Qaeda's ideology but infused with themes that resonate locally, increasing its salience, credibility, and audience acceptance. This hybridity has blurred the local and global, resulting in what has been termed "glocalization."[12] The distinction between the "far enemy," the United States and its allies, has been blurred with the "near enemy," the alleged apostate Muslim regimes. As Thomas Hegghammer comments:

> Al-Qaeda in Yemen is almost fully hybridized. Since 2006 it has launched numerous operations against both regime targets and western targets ... al-Qaeda in Yemen now has one of the most ambiguous enemy hierarchies in contemporary jihadism.[13]

According to AQAP, Muslims are suffering at the hands of a Crusader-Zionist alliance that props up illegitimate and corrupt local regimes that have failed to provide for their citizens. AQAP's diagnostic framework skillfully weaves local grievances into this wider narrative of persecution, marginalization, and threat. Appealing to tribal honor and deeply-felt religious sentiment, AQAP calls on

> ... the proud tribes of Yemen—people of support and victory—and the people of the Arabian Peninsula, to face the crusader campaign and their [collaborators] on the peninsula of Muhammad, prayer and peace upon him, [by] attacking their military bases, intelligence embassies, and their fleets that exist on the water and land of the Arabian Peninsula; until we stop the continuous massacres in the Muslim countries.[14]

This meta-narrative of suffering, which frequently focuses on issues of direct relevance to all Yemenis, such as events in Gaza and the Palestinian territories, is combined with grievances at the local level relating to inadequate service provision and inequities in natural resource allocation.

> The people of Yemen are suffering from the decline of their living standards, the rise of prices, and the discriminatory practices with which the government deals with them in employment, the distribution of wealth and its looting, the misappropriation of lands, and the absence of someone to defend their rights.[15]

AQAP has therefore attempted with considerable success to identify and instrumentalize pre-existing grievances. The organization's opportunistic support for the secessionist movement among tribes in southern Yemen must be seen in this light.

> This military movement mobilizing in Marib, Jawf, Shabwah, Abyan, Sana'a, and Hadramaut and which had been obscured in the media, is a step to strike the tribes with malicious excuses and shatter their pride, disarm them and control their lands, kill their sons, and make it easier for the bastard agents and the crusaders to humiliate them...[16]

AQAP has presented the Houthi insurgency in northern Yemen in a way that capitalizes on widespread fear of the rise of Shi'i Islam and Iranian influence. Like the government, which claims the Houthis seek to impose Shi'i religious law and accuses Iran of directing and financing the insurgency, AQAP portrays the insurgency in increasingly sectarian terms, which serve to undermine any claims of complicity between itself and the Houthis.

> If the Houthis were to win the war against the government, they would then have to deal with the Sunnis on numerous occasions that history will recall. We ask God to allow the defeat of the [Shi'i] rejectionists by the army and vice versa so that the Sunnis prevail.[17]

Addressing Grievances—AQAP's Prognostic Frame

> O youth of faith, toughen up and carry your weapons in the face of those who want to stand between you and the crusaders, those who want to sell you cheaply to their American masters and sacrifice you on the altar of Christians. Rise like one man to defend the dignities of your brothers in Afghanistan and Iraq who are fighting the Cross before us...[18]

Having tapped into a common grievance narrative, particularly targeted at a young, male demographic, AQAP offers a prognosis infused by the core al-Qaeda tenet of *d-wala' wal-bara'*—support for Muslims and enmity for non-Muslims. In the face of perceived injustice and proliferating existential threats, the prescription is violent jihad against the West and apostate Muslim regimes. The focus remains on ridding the Arabian Peninsula of all non-Muslims, the establishment of a local emirate, and the liberation of Palestine en route to the establishment of a global caliphate.[19]

Assessing the Threat—Capability and Intent

As stated repeatedly by the government of Yemen, there has been a marked tendency to exaggerate the threat posed by AQAP. A recent U.S. Senate report stated that "there are significant al-Qaeda populations in Yemen and Somalia."[20] However, estimates of the size of the group in Yemen vary from 300 to 500 to as many as several thousand.[21] The lower figure may represent active cadres within the organization, while the larger figure presumably includes supportive elements. This is a manageable, intelligence-led law enforcement task, with clear roles for external actors in the provision of intelligence, logistical support, and capacity-building. To what extent does AQAP's diagnostic and prognostic frame of reference resonate? For Sarah Phillips:

> Al-Qaeda in the Arabian Peninsula is presenting its credentials in the regime's stead, but is offering little more than a lightning rod for entrenched grievances, of which there are many.[22]

In addition, despite some tribal intermarriage designed to forge links between AQAP and tribal structures as well as consolidation in the governorates of Amran, Shabwa, Abyan, Hadramaut, and Marib, it is far from clear that AQAP will be able to exploit tribal discontent and rally tribes to the violent jihadi cause.

Phillips correctly finds that AQAP has succeeded in aligning its message with pre-existing grievances in Yemen. The organization's appeal to defensive mobilization in the face of actual and perceived threats is tailored to young men and Yemen's tribes. This process of mobilization, radicalization, and recruitment is frequently taking place in locations where individuals are temporarily distanced from supportive family and social networks, such as institutions of religious instruction. As with radicalization elsewhere, this is an inherently social process.[23] Estimates of the size of AQAP confirm its limited success at recruitment.

Despite its size, the organization has shown considerable capacity for organizational learning; for example, it has concentrated on the assassination of unpopular security force targets rather than large suicide bombings, realizing these are apt to alienate local communities. An educational focus is also evidenced by a section in *Sada al-Malahim* called the School of Yusuf (*Madrasat Yusif*), dedicated to such topics as how to resist interrogation. The magazine includes articles penned by the proselytization (*da'wa*), religious (*shari'a*), and military committees, indicators of AQAP's organizational structure.

Yemen as a Safe Haven and Destination for Foreign Fighters

Despite the limited membership of AQAP, it is necessary to separate the threat of radicalization in Yemen from the country's attraction as both a safe haven for other al-Qaeda elements and the threat posed by non-Yemenis gravitating to Yemen and then returning to their countries of origin to perpetrate attacks. For al-Qaeda, Yemen holds particular attractions as both a safe haven and a site of Islamic resurgence.

> The mountainous and immune landscape of Yemen has made this country a natural and secure fortress not only for the people of the Arabian Peninsula but for all the people of the Middle East. It is the stronghold that could provide shelter to the people and mujahideen of Yemen, and this has been a constant all through Yemen's military history.[24]

There have been increasing reports that al-Qaeda elements from the Pakistan/Afghanistan border area have started to move to Yemen. Al-Qaeda strategist Abu Musab al-Suri has highlighted the factors that make Yemen an attractive potential destination. The country comprises 75 percent of the population of the Arabian Peninsula and the "tribal coherent structure, the strength, the braveness, the love for fighting that the men of Yemen have—all this is an obvious historic fact since ancient times."[25] In addition, al-Suri claims there are 70 million small arms in the country[26] and notes its open borders, the proximity of the strategic Bab al-Mandab waterway, and

> ... the feelings of injustice and exploitation which are considered to be the main hidden motivator that must receive the right Islamic guidance in order to become an important strategic factor in motivating people towards jihad.[27]

While figures remain hard to verify, there are credible reports that Yemen is now a preferred destination for non-Yemeni converts or foreign fighters. Somalia is mentioned with increasing frequency in AQAP's media output, which along with offers of assistance from the armed Somali Islamist group al-Shabaab raises the specter of operational cooperation between the two groups. While cooperation may be just an aspiration at this stage, the presence of hundreds of thousands of Somali refugees in Yemen, established routes for smuggling people and weapons between Yemen and Somalia, and a shared strategic target in the Bab al-Mandab Strait separating the two counties make joint operational activity between the two groups highly likely. Geographical proximity augments the fact that both groups began to initiate attacks outside their immediate area of operations (AQAP in the United States, al-Shabaab in Australia and Denmark) in 2009.

The Limitations of Hard Power and a Developmental Approach to Counterterrorism

Military and law enforcement responses to the threat posed by AQAP clearly have a role to play. Such responses must be proportionate, exclusively Yemeni-led, and minimize the risk of civilian casualties, which would only serve to alienate communities that are the vital ground in governmental efforts to close down AQAP's operating space. The large number of civilian casualties following the al-Maajala airstrikes in Abyan simply reinforced the extremist narrative that the West is using its apostate government proxy to kill innocent Muslims. While there are concrete security measures that can and must be taken to address the AQAP threat, these cannot be considered in isolation. Given the considerable resonance between AQAP's diagnostic frame of reference and Yemeni grievances, there is a real risk this resonance will produce an increased receptivity or willingness to consider alternatives to traditional Yemeni ways of seeking redress, including violence. A comprehensive counterterrorism approach therefore goes beyond the application of hard power. Addressing the phenomenon of al-Qaeda in Saudi Arabia, Norman Cigar offers an analysis that applies equally to Yemen:

> The challenge of the socioeconomic grievances and opening up the system to greater participation, which might appeal to the pool of potential QAP [al-Qaeda in the Arabian Peninsula] sympathizers, remains to be dealt with, and that alone can ensure victory in the longer term over the QAP.[28]

Yemenis are focused on improving governmental responsiveness, accountability, service provision (particularly in relation to employment), and development. These are the keys to inoculating communities against al-Qaeda's violent prescriptions. The limited base of empirical evidence indicates that among many young people, support for armed groups—be they Houthi rebels in the North or AQAP—may be based more on economic considerations than deeply held ideological commitments. A developmental approach to countering the threat of terrorism in Yemen must focus on effective local participation, responsiveness, credibility and, crucially, service delivery. Al-Qaeda in the Arabian Peninsula is currently a localized threat with increasingly globalized ambitions. Addressing such a threat entails not simply kinetic counterterrorist initiatives but also a greater understanding of and attempt to address the points of resonance between the organization and local Yemeni communities, as well as the promotion of dissonance in relation to the means of seeking redress for actual and perceived grievances.

Recommendations

A. AVOID AN OVER-DEPENDENCE ON HARD POWER AND ADOPT A RADICALIZATION-SENSITIVE APPROACH. While targeted operations are necessary, they should be Yemeni-led, strenuously avoid civilian casualties that extremist narratives exploit, and should form part of a comprehensive partnership approach that prioritizes soft power and developmental initiatives so as to boost community resilience to violent radicalization. This would require the Yemeni government and its international partners to work with communities to identify and address needs. While mechanisms such as the governmental Social Fund for Development are available to aid this process, a responsive development assistance approach to counterterrorism can only succeed if accompanied by a genuine commitment by the government to address identified grievances. This will undercut AQAP's appeal to defensive mobilization in the face of what they identify as injustice, rampant corruption, and societal inequality.

B. MAP THE PUSH FACTORS THAT ARE SUPPORTING THE PROCESS OF RADICALIZATION. To understand the factors that push individuals into violent extremism, a systematic grievance mapping exercise should be undertaken with the Yemeni government. This would contain a geographical element, because support for AQAP is clustered in certain governorates (*muhafazat*). The objective of such an exercise would be, first, to reduce the salience of themes resonating between AQAP and Yemeni communities and, second, to exploit areas of dissonance, such as AQAP's rejection of dialogue, a central feature of traditional Yemeni means of dispute resolution.

C. UNDERSTAND WHAT AQAP IS SAYING AND HOW ITS MESSAGE RESONATES WITH YEMENI COMMUNITIES. Pull factors and the role of social networks and organizational dynamics are as important as push factors in understanding the process of radicalization. Such pull factors can also be elucidated from discussions with former members of AQAP as well as vulnerable individuals attracted by the organization's message, particularly young people.[29]

D. ANALYZE HOW AQAP DISSEMINATES ITS MESSAGE. This is of particular interest, given the low Internet penetration and high illiteracy rates in Yemen. Communication and network analysis should be utilized to address this lacuna. Core message themes should be disaggregated to highlight the varying levels of audience receptivity across demographics.

E. SUPPORT COUNTER-RADICALIZATION OR DE-RADICALIZATION INITIATIVES BASED ON DIALOGUE. The confrontation with al-Qaeda, both in Yemen and more broadly, is, in part, an ideological one, even if socialization and mobilization into terrorism often precede the religious framing of the conflict. Incidents of recidivism are an inevitable part of such programs, as they are among conventional prison populations, and should not be used to justify terminating such initiatives. What is required is a comprehensive analysis of the evolution and implementation of such programs around the world so as to inform creative new thinking.

F. INCLUDE THE ROLE OF WOMEN IN BOTH THE PROBLEM ANALYSIS AND THE EXPLORATION OF SOLUTIONS. Despite the understandable focus on the vulnerable young male population, it would be a mistake to focus interventions or development efforts on men only. AQAP's e-magazine *Sada al-Malahim* (The Echo of Epic Battles) places considerable emphasis on the role of women in jihad, and evidence from Saudi Arabia confirms that women are involved in the dissemination of al-Qaeda's message.[30]

G. ENSURE THAT EFFORTS TO ENHANCE THE CAPABILITY AND CAPACITY OF THE YEMENI SECURITY FORCES ARE MATCHED BY A CORRESPONDING FOCUS ON THEIR ACCOUNTABILITY AND ADHERENCE TO HUMAN RIGHTS NORMS. There is a significant risk that support of the Yemeni security forces may exacerbate existing grievances that fuel radicalization. In a 2008 U.S. Agency for International Development study on Yemeni youth, several individuals identified the security forces and the prison system as a factor in driving an individual towards violence. One individual stated, "Prisons and juvenile centers are supposed to rehabilitate the youth. What happens is the opposite. They get abused and they come out of jail even more aggressive and more violent."[31]

H. ADOPT A REGIONAL APPROACH. As the displacement of the al-Qaeda threat from Saudi Arabia to Yemen in 2009 highlights, a regional approach is required to effectively combat AQAP. Despite legitimate Western security fears, it should be remembered that the group poses the greatest threat to regional stability for the Gulf Cooperation Council (GCC) countries, and they should be encouraged to take the lead, even if the motivation for some is purely enlightened self-interest.

Notes

1. Hamil al-Misk, "Arba' Sanawat 'Ala al Najat wal Thabat" [Four Years after Survival and Steadfastness], *Sada al-Malahim*, vol. 12, February 2010, p. 35.

2. "Prince Muhammad bin Nayef Slightly Injured in Terrorist Attack," Royal Embassy of Saudi Arabia, Washington, D.C., August 28, 2009, http://www.saudiembassy.net/latest_news/news08280901.aspx.

3. "Amaliyat al-akh al-mujahid 'umar al-farouq al-nijiri fi rad al-'adwan al-amiriki 'ala al-yaman" [The operation of the mujahid'umar al-farouq the Nigerian in response to the American aggression on Yemen], al-Fajr Media Center; Steven Erlanger, "Nigerian May Have Used Course in Yemen as Cover," *New York Times*, January 1, 2009, http://www.nytimes.com/2010/01/01/world/middleeast/01yemen.html.

4. "US Giving Security Support to Yemen: Petraeus," David Petraeus interview, *Al Arabiya*, December 13, 2009, http://www.alarabiya.net/articles/2009/12/13/94083.html.

5. "U.S. Military Teams, Intelligence Deeply Involved in Aiding Yemen on Strikes," *Washington Post*, January 26, 2010, http://www.washingtonpost.com/wp-dyn/content/article/2010/01/26/AR2010012604239.html.

6. AQIY Leader Saeed al-Shehri: "Repelling the Crusader Aggression," February 8, 2010, http://www.nefafoundation.org/miscellaneous/Nefa_AQIY0210Tape.pdf.

7. Norman Cigar, *Al-Qa'ida's Doctrine for Insurgency* (Dulles, Va.: Potomac Books, 2009), p. 4.

8. Robert Benford and David Snow, "Framing Processes and Social Movements: An Overview and Assessment," *Annual Review of Sociology*, vol. 26, August 2000, pp. 611–639.

9. Testimony of Gregory D. Johnsen Before the Senate Foreign Relations Committee, January 20, 2010, http://foreign.senate.gov/testimony/2010/JohnsenTestimony100120a.pdf.

10. Murad Batal al-Shishani, *Terrorism Monitor*, vol. VIII, issue 9, March 5, 2010.

11. Personal communication with author, Sanaa, October 2009.

12. Roland Robertson, *Globalization: Social Theory and Global Culture* (London: Sage, 1994).

13. Thomas Hegghammer, "The Ideological Hybridization of Jihadi Groups," *Current Trends in Islamist Ideology*, vol. 9, 2009, p. 34.

14. "Al-Qaida in Yemen: AQIY Responds to Airstrike with New Threats," December 27, 2009, NEFA Foundation, http://www.nefafoundation.org/miscellaneous/nefaAQIYresponse1209.pdf.

15. Hamil al-Misk, "Min huna nabda . . ." [From Here We Start . . .], *Sada al-Malahim*, vol. 8, March 2009, p. 27.

16. Nasser al-Wahayshi, "Wa yamkurun wa yamkur Allah" [And the unbelievers plotted and planned, and Allah too planned], *Sada al-Malahim*, vol. 8, March 2009, p. 5.

17. Sheikh Ibrahim al-Rubaysh, "Al-al-rawafid wa marahil al-muwajaha" [The Rejectionists and the Stages of Confrontation], *Sada al-Malahim*, vol. 11, October 2009, pp. 25–26.

18. Abu Hajer al-Muqrin,"Risala Ila Shabab al-Yaman" [A Letter to the Youth of Yemen], *Sada al-Malahim*, vol. 4, July 2008, p. 38.

19. See http://www.aawsat.com/details.asp?section=4&article=559187&issueno=11416.

20. *Al Qaeda in Yemen and Somalia: A Ticking Time Bomb* (2010), Report of the U.S. Senate Committee on Foreign Relations, http://foreign.senate.gov/imo/media/doc/Yemen.pdf, p. 8.

21. While most estimates place the membership at 300–500, Yemeni journalist Abdalilah Haydar Shay'a, who has interviewed senior members of the organization, places membership at 3,000, http://www.aawsat.com/details.asp?section=4&article=559187&issueno=11416.

22. Sarah Phillips, *What Comes Next in Yemen: Al-Qaeda, the Tribes, and State-Building*, http://www.carnegieendowment.org/files/yemen_tribes.pdf, p. 7.

23. Marc Sageman, *Understanding Terror Networks* (Philadelphia: University of Pennsylvania Press, 2004). On radicalization in the Middle East see R. Hutson, T. Long, and M. Page, "Pathways to Violent Radicalization in the Middle East—A Model for Future Studies of Transnational Jihad," *Royal United Services Institute Journal*, 154/2, 2009, pp. 18–26.

24. Abu Musab al-Suri, "The Responsibility of the People of Yemen Regarding the Sanctuary of Muslims," http://www.tawhed.ws/r?i=wksgfnyz.

25. Ibid.

26. More recent studies have estimated the number of weapons in Yemen at the significantly reduced but still extremely high figure of 6–9 million. Derek B. Miller, "Demand, Stockpiles, and Social Controls: Small Arms in Yemen," Small Arms Survey, Occasional Paper no. 9, May 2003, http://www.smallarmssurvey.org/files/sas/publications/o_papers_pdf/2003-op09-yemen.pdf.

27. Ibid.

28. Cigar, op. cit., p. 51.

29. John Horgan, *Walking Away From Terrorism: Accounts of Disengagement from Radical and Extremist Movements* (New York: Routledge, 2008).

30. Cigar, op. cit., footnote 69.

31. USAID, *Yemen Cross-Sectoral Youth Assessment* (Washington D.C.: USAID, 2008), p. 35. Cited in Alistair Harris and Michael Page "Al-Qa'ida in Yemen: Situation Update and Recommendations for Policy Makers," http://www.rusi.org/analysis/commentary/ref:C4B475DF54843E.

WAR IN SAADA: FROM LOCAL INSURRECTION TO NATIONAL CHALLENGE

Christopher Boucek

Since 2004 the Yemeni government has been mired in a militarily unwinnable, sporadic civil conflict against the Houthis, a group of Shi'i Zaidi revivalists in the northern governorate of Saada. The war has had a disproportionate toll on noncombatants and has led to a widespread humanitarian crisis: More than 250,000 people have been displaced, and significant civilian infrastructure has been destroyed. There is no good data on casualties, but estimates of the number killed range from several hundred to several thousand. The war has not improved security and stability in Yemen; rather, it has exposed greater vulnerabilities for the regime, weakened the central government, and emboldened other threatening actors such as al-Qaeda. However, the most severe threat to Yemen is its economic crisis, which the conflict's financial costs have rapidly accelerated. Conditions went from bad to worse in November 2009 when Saudi Arabia's military entered the conflict, internationalizing what had been a domestic conflict.

Yemen faces daunting, interconnected challenges: a failing economy, massive unemployment, runaway population growth, resource exhaustion, a rapidly falling water table, dwindling state capacity, an inability to deliver social services throughout much of the country, and interwoven corruption and governance issues. The Houthi conflict exacerbates these challenges, as do a growing secessionist movement in the former South Yemen and a resurgent al-Qaeda organization. The war in Saada takes precedence over concurrent security challenges such as confronting al-Qaeda in the Arabian Peninsula (AQAP) and resolving secessionist aspirations in the South.

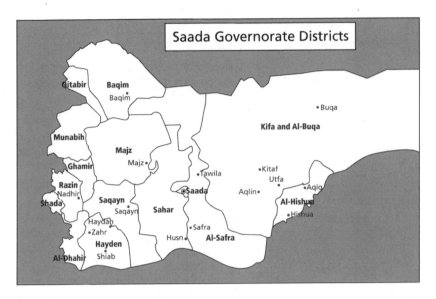

The government's tacit support of hard-line Salafi activists in Saada has diluted Zaidi influence there. The Houthi rebels are protesting this dilution as well as the historic underdevelopment of the governorate. The government has accused the Houthis of seeking to establish a Shi'i theocracy in Saada and wanting to revive the Zaidi imamate that ruled for nearly a thousand years until being overthrown in the 1962 republican revolution. In actuality, the conflict arose from a complex combination of competing sectarian identities, regional underdevelopment, perceived socioeconomic injustices, and historical grievances.[1] It is exacerbated by tensions between the indigenous Zaidi Shi'i population and Sunni Salafi fundamentalists who have relocated to the area. Tribal rivalries also complicate matters, because the regime has recruited tribal fighters to combat the insurrection.

The Yemeni government has sought to link the rebellion to the larger "war on terrorism" and garner international support by claiming the Houthis' supporters include secular Libya, radical Sunni extremist al-Qaeda, Lebanese Hizbollah, and Shi'i Iran. The state has not yet produced evidence that the Houthi rebels are receiving outside military assistance, or proven its recent assertions that Iran is meddling in the conflict.

The war grew more dangerous in November 2009 when Saudi Arabia openly entered the fighting. Riyadh, responding to Houthi incursions, launched a major military operation on its southern border—the first unilateral Saudi military operation in decades. Some analysts have expressed concern that Saudi involvement in the Houthi conflict might prompt Iran to follow suit, adding a dangerous international dimension to the war. Saudi Arabia's actions have compounded the complexity of the situation and dramatically complicated future international mediation efforts.

In the long term the Saada war is not the most immediate security threat to the country; that title goes to the growing challenge of the southern secessionist movement, which imperils Yemeni territorial integrity and the current Yemeni government. National unity has been an overriding preoccupation for the regime since Yemen's 1990 unification and the 1994 civil war to prevent separation. Much of Yemen's hydrocarbon resources, as well as the natural deepwater port of Aden, are in the south, so the prospect of half the country splitting off is perceived as a direct threat to the country's economy. The government considers the energy resources and port as possible future sources of income, although hydrocarbon resources are quickly running out. Secession would threaten the national economy but, more ominously for leaders in Sanaa, directly challenge the ruling order; the government has taken a zero-tolerance policy on secession. The Southern Movement is the biggest threat to Yemeni stability in the long run, but the regime is most involved in Saada for two key reasons: first, Yemen's leaders view the war in Saada as winnable, and second, the government uses its military operations in the North to send a message of resolve to southern agitators for secession.

Neither the rebels nor the government can expect a military solution to the conflict after nearly six years of fighting. A grinding status quo has emerged, characterized by ongoing low-level hostilities that periodically escalate into larger bouts of sustained and prolonged fighting. These rounds of fighting—there have been six—are especially brutal and indiscriminate, and local civilian populations have suffered greatly. The Yemeni army is untrained and unequipped to fight a classic counterinsurgency campaign and has increasingly relied on indirect fire, artillery, and airpower. The Houthis have been accused of indiscriminate, brutal methods that have increased civilian casualties, destroyed infrastructure, and resulted in more than 250,000 internally displaced persons. The misery in Saada is compounded by reported food blockades, and there are allegations that the government repeatedly has cut off telephone and other communications there.

Rumors of shadowy arms deals and other nebulous financial transactions frequently circulate in Yemen, as do claims that regime figures have used the conflict and related arm sales for their personal enrichment. Such stories are notoriously difficult to verify, yet they contribute to the confusion that surrounds the war in Saada. There is some talk that the fighting in Saada is complicated by struggles to determine a successor for President Ali Abdullah Saleh, who came to power in 1978. There are reports of clashes between General Ali Mohsin, the commander of the northern military district, and Ahmed Ali Abdullah Saleh, the president's son and commander of the Republican Guard. Again, such rumors are extremely difficult to confirm; however, a look at the major regime personalities prosecuting the war in Saada helps explain why such stories are repeated so frequently.

Understanding Saada and Zaidism

The governorate of Saada is along Yemen's northern border with Saudi Arabia. Saada historically has suffered from underdevelopment and was among the last Yemeni regions incorporated into the republic. The central government in Sanaa has had a greater presence in other portions of the country; it does not have full control of Saada (nor of other parts of the country). Some analyses suggest that portions of Saada have never been under central government control but are governed by local authorities. Saada is among Yemen's poorest governorates and receives little in the way of civil services: It is one of the few governorates where the Water Ministry has not established a local water corporation. However, the regime has not completely ignored it: Recent official figures show Saada receives approximately 12 percent of all water subsidies (second after Sanaa, which received 48 percent).

The government is fighting Shi'i Zaidi revivalists, who were originally fighting to protest the dilution of Zaidi identity and influence. Most Yemenis follow the Shafi school of Sunni Islam; only 35 percent to 40 percent of Yemenis are Zaidis, and most members of this school live in Yemen. Zaidism frequently is viewed as a Sunni school of Shi'ism and Shafism as a Shi'i school of Sunnism.[2] Zaidism is a very small subset of the global Shi'i community, and in practice it is very similar to Sunni Islam. It is doctrinally different from the more common "Twelver Islam" practiced in Iran and elsewhere. This leads many observers to doubt that Tehran would support the Houthis.

The role of the imam is central to traditional Zaidi belief. Zaidi doctrine holds that the leader of the community, the *imam*, must be a *sayyid*, or descendant of the Prophet Mohammed through his daughter Fatimah. A Shi'i Zaidi imamate governed Yemen for nearly a thousand years, until the revolution of 1962. Following the overthrow of this monarchy, the status of Yemen's Zaidi community—and in particular that of the Zaidi *sayyids*—declined dramatically. Today's Yemeni Zaidi community appears divided on the need for an imam. Indeed, the current absence of an imam is a key aspect of contemporary Zaidism in Yemen, and it underscores a central government argument that Houthis seek to revive the imamate under their own leadership.

The current reasons for the war in Saada bear little resemblance to the causes of the initial outbreak of fighting in 2004. Then, the conflict was driven by a sense of sectarian marginalization, economic underdevelopment, and displeasure at governmental policies on cooperation with the United States and Saudi Arabia. Today the war is about broader anger and dissatisfaction with the Saleh regime. Throughout the conflict, the Houthi leadership has been very careful to not identify many specific demands. While this can in part be attributed to a calculated attempt to not get pinned down by the government, it also demonstrates the leadership's lack of unity and a coherent vision. Today, it seems that the primary Houthi position is opposition to the central government, and the movement's *raison d'être* is resistance to Yemeni military offensives.

This transformation—and the movement away from demands—have greatly complicated any resolution to the conflict. As the Congressional Research Service noted in a recent report, the conflict has "transformed from an ideological/religious revival movement into more of a classical insurgency."[3] One analyst, writing during the recent sixth round of fighting, observed that

> ... the insurgency is more a reaction to a dysfunctional government than an inspired, centralized, ideological movement. Although there is a core of ideologically motivated fighters, most members do not appear to have any kind of consistent national or international objective.... the Houthi leadership has portrayed its position as purely defensive against the acts of state oppression and attacks by the Yemeni army.[4]

Lack of Reliable Information

Throughout the war in Saada, several factors have made it extremely difficult to obtain accurate information about conditions there. This has severely complicated outside analyses of the conflict. The Yemeni government has severely restricted reporting from Saada and has prosecuted several reporters and media organizations on dubious allegations of supporting the insurrection. Fighting and government restrictions have meant foreign media have little access to Saada, so the majority of reporting is based on two sources: the official state media and the Houthi rebels. Both have incentives to report favorable and distorted interpretations of the conflict; this has been the norm throughout the rebellion. International humanitarian and relief organizations have also suffered from a lack of access. However, in the past year there have been several very thorough reports.[5] This has improved the outside understanding of the situation in Saada, but many questions remain.

The Six Rounds of Conflict

Round 1: June 2004 to September 2004

The armed conflict began in 2004 following anti-government demonstrations by members of the Believing Youth (*Shabab al-Mumin*) movement, which originated in the early 1990s as an informal advocacy group for Zaidi education and culture. The group was tolerated, and even supported, by Saleh and the government to counter the growth of Salafism in Yemen.[6]

In 2004 militants associated with the group disrupted mosque services in Saada, shouting anti-government, anti-American, and anti-Israeli slogans. The disturbances soon spread to Sanaa, with protesters criticizing the Saleh regime for its counterterrorism cooperation with the United States. Exact details are difficult to come by, but reports suggest that some 600 Zaidi protesters were detained in Sanaa following the outbursts. That June, after an unsuccessful reconciliation effort, the government attempted to arrest Believing Youth leader Hussein Badr al-din al-Houthi, a former member of parliament representing the al-Haqq party. The government accused him of fomenting unrest and seeking to revive the Zaidi imamate.

Government forces clashed with Houthi rebels throughout June, with reports of fierce fighting in Marran and Haydan. Government rhetoric against the Houthis escalated, including allegations that the group sought to "incite sectarianism" and spread "extremism" and "deviancy."[7] The fighting continued into July, when the government offered a bounty of 10 million Yemeni riyal ($55,000) on al-Houthi. During July, the government deployed more forces to Saada and began to link the Houthis to Iran and Hizbollah — a charge the Houthis swiftly rejected. Al-Houthi countered that he and his movement were loyal to Yemen but opposed the government's close cooperation with the United States and Saudi Arabia's involvement in domestic affairs. By September more government forces were deployed in Saada, and the conflict continued to escalate. Hussein al-Houthi was killed in early September, leading the government to proclaim unilateral victory in Saada and the defeat of the Houthi rebels. This marked the end of what has been termed the first round of fighting; Yemeni press reports that more than 1,000 civilians died in this round. However, since September 2004, the al-Houthi family has led five additional rounds of fighting.

Round 2: March 2005 to May 2005

Hussein al-Houthi's father, Badr al-Din al-Houthi, assumed leadership of the movement following Hussein's death. The Yemeni government charged Badr al-Din al-Houthi, a noted Zaidi scholar, and Abdullah al-Ruzami, a former member of parliament from the al-Haqq party, with resuming the insurgency. Al-Ruzami countered that Yemeni President Ali Abdullah Saleh did not want the conflict to end. After a series of skirmishes, the conflict escalated in late March with heavy fighting taking place in Majz, Sahar, Baqim, and Dahyan. Saleh accused two political parties—al-Haqq and the Union of Popular Forces—of supporting the rebellion, charging them with terrorism against the government, the military, and attempts to kidnap ambassadors to Yemen. According to reports, Saleh appeared on television in May to pardon Badr al-Din al-Houthi, although during this time other prominent Houthi supporters were tried and convicted on charges of espionage and insurrection.[8] According to press reports, Badr al-Din rejected the pardon offer. Saleh reportedly used the anniversary of the 1962 republican revolution to declare an amnesty for Houthi prisoners, although it seems that many remained in detention. In May 2005, the government again announced a unilateral victory and declared an end to hostilities. However, sporadic fighting continued.

Round 3: November 2005 to Early 2006

This round began with tribal fighting between the pro-government Hamdan tribe of Sheikh Abdullah al-Awjari and tribes supporting the Houthi rebels. In late 2005 government forces began heavy fighting in Saada. The government also released a large number of Houthi detainees, although others reportedly were put on trial. In early 2006 Houthi rebels were accused of attempting to assassinate a Ministry of Justice official in Dhamar, south of Sanaa.[9] The elderly Badr al-Din al-Houthi reportedly died of natural causes in February 2005, and two of his sons, Abdul Malik al-Houthi and Yahya al-Houthi, assumed leadership of the rebellion, which has continued under the leadership of Abdul Malik. Yahya, a former member of parliament from the ruling General People's Congress party, is currently in exile in Germany and has served as one of the movement's spokesmen.

The government was pressured to end the fighting before voting began for the September 20, 2006, presidential and municipal elections. Saleh amnestied some 600 prisoners, including Mohammed Badr al-Din al-Houthi, and announced a new governor for Saada in an effort to end the fighting. It was also reported that Saleh ordered that government forces hand over the home of Hussein al-Houthi and that the Houthi family receive a government salary.[10] This relative lull, however, would not last.

Round 4: January 2007 to June 2007

The government maintains this round was sparked in part by Houthi threats against the indigenous Jewish community in Saada. Fighting quickly escalated, spreading throughout Saada and into neighboring governorates. Government allegations of Iranian and Libyan support for the Houthis resurfaced, and Sanaa recalled its ambassadors from Tehran and Tripoli; Houthi leaders denied these charges of foreign intervention. In February 2007 the Yemeni government sought to extradite Yahya al-Houthi from Libya, where he had sought refuge; Yahya travelled to Germany and sought political asylum. During this time, according to Reuters News Agency, the Yemeni government stripped Yahya al-Houhti of his parliamentary immunity and began to actively recruit tribal levies to deploy in Saada. This significant development permanently altered the complexion of the conflict: Introducing tribal fighters has added new layers of complexity to the conflict, injecting tribal politics into what had thus far been a largely sectarian conflict. This shift would prove to be a lasting factor of subsequent fighting, as the war in Saada metastasized.

Qatari mediation ended this fourth round. In May 2007 Qatari Emir Hamad visited Yemen, and a delegation from the Qatari foreign ministry met with the Houthi leadership. Shortly thereafter Yahya al-Houthi traveled to Qatar. Following these meetings, a list of general principles was created, which led to a cease-fire in mid-June 2007. The Qatari peace plan, called the Doha Agreement, was initially kept secret. It included several broad components, including a government amnesty, the reconstruction of Saada, a commitment by the Houthis to give up their heavy weapons, and the establishment of a committee to work out the specifics of a peace settlement. That committee comprised representatives from the Yemeni government, the Houthis, and the Qatari government. The subsequent agreement included a halt to all military operations, the release of all prisoners within one month, and the establishment of committees to handle compensation and reconstruction. It also called for senior Houthi leaders including Abdul Malik al-Houthi, Abdul Karim al-Houthi, and Abdullah al-Ruzami to go into permanent exile in Qatar. These were important first steps, although fighting in Saada persisted throughout this process.

Despite this progress the Doha Agreement failed, because it provided no specifics on how to reconstruct Saada or arrange the exile of the senior Houthi leaders, and because of Saudi displeasure at Qatar's involvement. The Yemeni government also complained that the Qatari mediation efforts led the Houthis to believe that they were equal to the state. The agreement collapsed, but its fundamentals remain the likely basis for any future settlement.

Round 5: March 2008 to July 2008

Sporadic fighting continued from summer 2007 until March 2008, when the fifth round of fighting broke out. Conditions seriously deteriorated, and fighting spread beyond Saada, reaching Bani Hushaysh on the northern outskirts of Sanaa. The fighting steadily intensified until Saleh declared a unilateral cease-fire on July 17, 2008—the thirtieth anniversary of his rule. The Yemeni Republican Guard saw combat, and tribal militias fought on behalf of the government.

According to some reports, the proximity of the fighting to Sanaa led to concern among regime elites. According to the Congressional Research Service, during this time there were also rumors of an "aborted coup and shakeups within the military."[11] Saleh was rumored to have sought a cease-fire for several reasons: international pressure, the scale of the humanitarian toll, local mediation, and concern about the proximity of the rebel advance.

In March 2009 tensions again began to rise. Throughout the spring and summer, violent clashes came more frequently, and in June 2009 nine foreign aid workers were abducted in Saada governorate. The bodies of the three female victims were discovered several days later; they apparently had been executed shortly after the kidnapping. The level of violence and absence of any conditions for releasing the captives distinguished this abduction from previous kidnappings. It was more like al-Qaeda-style abductions, such as those seen in Iraq and Pakistan. It has been suggested by some observers that Islamist militants staged the kidnapping in Saada to provoke the Yemeni government into restarting the war in Saada and to divert focus from AQAP.

Round 6: August 2009 Through February 2010

The kidnappings set the stage for this most recent round of the Saada war, which followed rebel closures of several key roads, including the road linking Saada and Sanaa. The Yemeni government started this round by launching Operation Scorched Earth in August 2009.

Operation Scorched Earth

President Saleh asserted that the Houthis would be handled once and for all, and declared the regime's resolve to crush the rebellion with an "iron fist." Despite early promises to swiftly defeat the Houthis, this latest round of fighting deteriorated into consistent and ongoing fighting. A month into the government offensive, the Houthis had seized Baqim and al-Safra districts in Saada, and fighting had spread to Harf Sufyan district in neighboring Amran governorate. Several cease-fires were declared, but none has lasted.

According to a January 2010 report in *Jane's Intelligence Review*, the Yemeni government has deployed more than 40,000 soldiers in support of Operation Scorched Earth. This represents a major increase from previous episodes. Fighting in previous rounds had spilled out of Saada, but the war further metastasized during Operation Scorched Earth through the potent combination of tribalization and indiscriminate fire. The government has also deployed the Popular Army, an amalgam of tribal levies and informal fighters. Tribal rivalries are playing out in the theater, leading to violence and fighting unrelated to the actual war. Reports of tribal fighting include conflicts between the Shaker and Sufiyan tribes of the Bakil tribal confederation; between Kharef and other tribes of the Hashid tribal confederation; and between the Najar and al-Farhan tribes.

Previous rounds of fighting have included indiscriminate fire, but the sixth round increasingly has featured government artillery and aerial bombardments. Such tactics disproportionately target noncombatants, increase civilian collateral damage, and increase local animosity to the central government.

According to local Yemeni sources, the government's decision to relaunch the war in Saada was driven by a perception that the regime could finally vanquish the Houthi rebels. The central government likely also was driven by a desire to reopen roads from Sanaa to Saada closed by the Houthis. It is probable that the Yemeni government sought to use the war in Saada as an example for southern secessionists.

It is extremely unlikely that Sanaa would have begun military operations without consulting Riyadh and other regional actors. Saudi Arabia allegedly has helped finance the recent fighting, and it is likely that the Saudis provided some international political cover for the Yemeni government. For several months after Operation Scorched Earth began in August 2009, there was surprisingly little international criticism of the war. On the contrary, the Gulf Cooperation Council voiced its support for Yemen (and later Saudi Arabia) as the government sought to contain the Houthis. A number of Sunni Arab countries have lobbied in Washington to encourage support of the Yemeni government's military action.

The Current Cease-Fire

A cease-fire was reached in mid-February 2010, ending immediate hostilities in Saada. As of this writing, the cease-fire holds. However, the government shows no interest in addressing the underlying causes of the war, which is now six years old, or the grievances that have perpetuated the conflict. The sixth round of fighting in Saada was dramatically more violent than earlier rounds, and the current cease-fire can in part be explained by exhaustion on both sides. Based on recent field research in Yemen, it is likely that the current lull in violence will last longer than previous interludes, in larger part due to mutual exhaustion. Nonetheless, because nothing has been done to resolve the grievances at the heart of the conflict, it is also extremely likely that fighting will resume. Some sources claim that the Houthis have stockpiled enough arms for another two years of fighting.

Throughout the conflict, the Houthis have complained that the expansion of Sunni Salafi beliefs, propagated in part in schools, dilutes Zaidi culture and identity. Houthi leaders allege that the central government has been complicit in this process. Senior Yemeni government officials have noted that the government is prepared to acquiesce on certain Houthi demands, including the establishment of a Zaidi university in Saada and the creation of a political party; it is more circumspect on changing the national school curriculum. Yemeni officials claim they cannot unilaterally change a national curriculum; that would require action in the Ministry of Education and other agencies.

The growing radicalization among elements of the Houthi movement further complicates matters. According to local analyses, some rebels consider having survived recent Yemeni and Saudi military operations as a Houthi victory. Local observers fear that such interpretations might embolden further Houthi attacks against the Yemeni government and encourage some rebel elements to expand military operations with the aim of overthrowing the regime. This marks a major deterioration: The Houthis previously had never made any claims outside of Saada. This worrisome development underscores the need for immediate steps to defuse tensions and minimize violence in Saada.

A Proxy Conflict?

There is no evidence that Operation Scorched Earth is a proxy conflict between Sunni Saudi Arabia and Shi'i Iran. There are more than enough grievances in Yemen and Saada to perpetuate the fighting without drawing in regional dynamics. Saudi Arabia has supported the Yemeni government in war, but a Saudi–Iranian regional rivalry is not playing out in Saada. However, Saudi military operations on the Yemeni border—and Saudi forces' inability to defeat the Houthis—might lead Iran to play a more provocative role in Saada in order to pressure Saudi Arabia.

The Yemeni government has never produced any evidence to support its allegations that Tehran is supporting the Houthis; in fact, some Yemeni officials have confided that such assertions are unfounded. No Iranians have been killed or captured in Saada, and proof of Iranian weapons transfers never has been produced. The Iranian government and state media have been supportive of the Houthis, and it is likely that some private Iranians have informally funded the insurgency. However, this is far from official Iranian government support for Hizbollah, Hamas, and Iraqi insurgents. Some low-level representatives from the Ministry of Intelligence and Security or Revolutionary Guards might have meddled in Saada in an ad hoc fashion; however, such interference is neither official nor sustained.

Saudi Involvement

In early November 2009, Saudi Arabia openly entered the conflict with significant military operations against the Houthis. The action followed persistent rumors of clandestine Saudi military operations on the border against Houthi rebels. The Saudi offensive followed reports of Houthi incursions in Saudi territory that killed several Saudi border guards.

In the days preceding the Saudi offensive, the Yemeni military was allowed to transit through Saudi territory in order to flank Houthi rebel positions. Perhaps the Houthi leadership intended to internationalize the conflict by shooting at Saudi border guards. That gunfire also might have been an attempt to punish the Saudis for their tacit cooperation with the Yemeni government. On the other hand, the Saudi involvement might have been an unintended escalation. The Saudi–Yemen border is not well-demarcated, and armed Houthi guerrillas might have crossed the border unwittingly, provoking a confrontation with Saudi border guards anxious to keep out infiltrators.

The resulting Saudi military response clearly was preplanned, not reactionary. Its swiftness suggests that Saudi forces were prepared to respond, needing only a pretext—such as the attack on a Saudi border post—for action. Saudi officials had expressed concern about deteriorating conditions in Yemen for some time before the incursion and reportedly had established a Special Forces unit specializing in mountain warfare on its southern border.

The Saudis consider Yemen a major security challenge. Significant numbers of Saudi militants (including eleven Guantanamo returnees[12]) have fled to Yemen since AQAP established itself there, and they pose a growing threat to the kingdom. In August 2009 one such Saudi national returned to the kingdom and tried to assassinate Saudi counterterrorism chief Prince Mohammed bin Nayef.

A Serious Threat to Stability

The fighting in Saada has done little to advance stability or security in Yemen. The humanitarian and financial costs have been enormous, yet conditions on the ground make these costs impossible to accurately discern. Prosecuting the war has hampered the Yemeni military's effectiveness, preoccupied the central government to the exclusion of nearly every other issue, led to widespread humanitarian suffering, and rapidly accelerated the country's economic crisis.

Over the course of the six-year conflict, nearly every aspect of the Yemeni military has seen combat in Saada, including the Central Security Force Counter-Terrorism Unit. Some analyses maintain that the only units that have not been deployed to Saada are the regime defense and personal protection units—in itself a very telling fact. The toll on the Yemeni armed forces has been significant, with reports of desertions, falling morale, and allegations of black market sales of state munitions and materiel. The required post-deployment re-equipping and refitting is a cost that the Yemeni government can little afford. This strain on the military has led to questions about its ability to simultaneously engage in other operations such as combating Islamist extremism, fighting AQAP, and extending state control throughout the country.

The government's failure to decisively put down the rebellion has prompted concerns that other domestic challengers might be emboldened and perceive the regime as vulnerable. Islamist militants or other disaffected groups could mount attacks on other fronts while the government is distracted in Saada. The longer that the war in Saada goes on, the weaker the central government appears. Yet some Yemeni officials have argued that stopping hostilities would show weakness and a lack of state resolve.

The humanitarian toll has been significant. The war has produced an estimated 250,000 internally displaced persons in Saada, Amran, Hajja, and Sanaa; most were displaced during the most recent round of fighting. Relief organizations have complained about a lack of access and the difficulty in delivering supplies to those most affected.

The war in Saada's greatest consequence has been its devastation of the Yemeni economy. The war has consumed many resources, dramatically accelerating the nation's financial crisis. All other challenges facing the country are linked to the economy. Previous assessments had suggested that Yemen's economic crisis was several years in the future, but the costly war effort has accelerated the timetable. Sanaa has been spending money it does not have to finance the war, and every riyal spent on the war effort is a riyal that is not spent on delivering human services, ensuring food security, or combating AQAP. By some estimates, the central government has spent more than $1 billion in hard currency reserves during the sixth round of fighting; this figure does not include subsidies from the Saudis and other countries. Estimates of this year's budget deficit range from 9 percent to 23 percent, and it is unclear how the Yemeni government can meet this shortfall without foreign assistance. Despite new natural gas revenues and royalties, oil exports continue to decrease and state income is falling. Roughly 80 percent of the Yemeni budget is salaries, pensions, and diesel subsidies—areas off limits to any cuts. As the economy deteriorates, every other problem worsens and Sanaa's ability to manage concurrent crises decreases.

The war in Saada has received little international attention, despite the widespread humanitarian toll. U.S. and Western concerns vis-à-vis Yemen focus solely on al-Qaeda and international terrorism. The Houthis do not threaten Western interests, so the international community has been little concerned with the deteriorating situation in Saada. For the Yemeni government, however, the war in Saada has been all-consuming.

The regime and republic face an existential threat from the Houthi rebellion and southern secessionist movement. Both conflicts illustrate the fraying of the Yemeni state. The government's uncompromising position in Saada has exacerbated local grievances and rapidly accelerated Yemen's economic crisis. Neither the Yemeni government nor the Houthis can de-escalate the conflict at this point, and there is no political will to end the war. Doing so will require foreign intervention, but no foreign actors are inclined to act. Given the level of tensions, further fighting is likely.

Notes

1. "Yemen: Defusing the Saada Time Bomb," Middle East Report no. 6, Brussels: International Crisis Group, 2009.

2. See Greg Johnsen remarks at the Carnegie Endowment for International Peace event, "Al-Qaeda in Yemen," July 7, 2009, http://www.carnegieendowment.org/events/?fa=eventDetail&id=1372; International Crisis Group, "Yemen: Defusing the Saada Time Bomb," May 27, 2009, http://www.crisisgroup.org/home/index.cfm?action=login&ref_id=6113; Laurent Bonnefoy, "Varieties of Islamism in Yemen: The Logic of Integration Under Pressure," *Middle East Review of International Affairs*, vol. 13, no. 1, March 2009.

3. Jeremy M. Sharp, "Yemen: Background and U.S. Relations," CRS Report for Congress, Washington, D.C.: Congressional Research Service, January 13, 2010.

4. Joost Hilterman, "Disorder on the Border: Saudi Arabia's War Inside Yemen," *Foreign Affairs*, December 16, 2009.

5. See ICG, "Yemen: Defusing the Saada Time Bomb," J. E. Peterson, "The al-Huthi Conflict in Yemen," Arabian Peninsula Background Note, no. APBN-006, published on www.jepeterson.net, August 2008; Michael Horton, "Borderline Crisis: Saudi Arabia Intervenes in Yemen," *Jane's Intelligence Review*, January 2010; Jack Freeman, "The al-Houthi Insurgency in the North of Yemen: An Analysis of the Shabab al Moumineen," *Studies in Conflict & Terrorism* vol. 32, no. 11, November 11, 2009.

6. Michael Horton, "Borderline Crisis: Saudi Arabia Intervenes in Yemen," *Jane's Intelligence Review*, January 2010, p. 13.

7. J. E. Peterson, "The al-Huthi Conflict in Yemen," Arabian Peninsula Background Note, no. APBN-006, published on www.jepeterson.net, August 2008, p. 5.

8. Peterson, "The al-Huthi Conflict in Yemen," p. 8.

9. Ibid.

10. Peterson, "The al-Huthi Conflict in Yemen," p. 9.

11. Jeremy M. Sharp, "Yemen: Background and U.S. Relations," CRS Report for Congress, Washington, D.C.: Congressional Research Service, January 13, 2010, p. 18.

12. Only eight of the eleven Guantanamo detainees believed to be hiding out in Yemen are thought to remain at large.

THE POLITICAL CHALLENGE OF YEMEN'S SOUTHERN MOVEMENT

Stephen Day

Three opposition groups threaten the stability of Yemen, and possibly its survival within its current borders. The two more menacing groups—al-Qaeda in the Arabian Peninsula (AQAP) and the armed Houthi rebellion—have received the lion's share of international attention. But foreign observers should look more closely at the third, the Southern Movement, which has recently been undergoing a radical transformation. When the Southern Movement surfaced in 2007, its demands were moderate: equality with citizens in the nation's North; jobs; greater local decision-making power; and more control over the South's economic resources, including Yemen's largest oil field at al-Maseela in Hadramaut province. Today, some elements within the Southern Movement are urging secession from Yemen and reestablishment of an independent South Yemen (or what is called "South Arabia" by those more virulently opposed to the 1990 unification with Yemenis in the North). Recent developments also hint that the Southern Movement is developing ties with al-Qaeda, even though the former had a different origin with different goals pursued by peaceful and democratic means.

The Southern Movement started as a reaction to the mishandling of Yemen's unification over the past two decades. This unity process failed to solve basic problems of national identity, economic development, and political governance. Many in the South believe President Ali Abdullah Saleh, his family, and his Hashid tribe have discriminated against them while exploiting the South's resources for personal gain. At its outset, the Southern Movement represented a political challenge to the regime. But if domestic problems continue to be mishandled, the Southern Movement might threaten the state, particularly if its members cooperate with al-Qaeda. Last year Nasser al-Wahayshi, the leader of AQAP, declared support for the Southern Movement and its goal of secession, expressing his hopes to see an independent Islamic state in the South, where AQAP could establish a new base of operations.[1] Al-Wahayshi does not set the agenda of the Southern Movement, and there is no evidence that southern leaders share his dream of an Islamic state, but the Southern Movement clearly challenges Yemen's political status quo, risking greater instability. This presents a dilemma for policy makers. On the one hand, the instability resulting from the Southern Movement's activities creates an environment in which AQAP can deepen its roots and grow strong, especially if the Southern Movement becomes more radical. On the other hand, if the Southern Movement is conflated with al-Qaeda and military force is used to repress its civilian supporters, there is an equal or greater risk of magnifying AQAP's role in the South and worsening the problem of terrorism emanating from Yemen.

A Mishandled Unification Process

Across history Yemenis rarely have been unified under common rule. The country's geography—tall mountains in the West around the capital Sanaa, a large interior desert, and a remarkable canyon system in the East known as Wadi Hadramaut—created and perpetuated divisions in pre-Islamic times. In the Islamic period distinct religious schools and ruling systems emerged. Zaidis, followers of a minor Shi'i school of Islam, dominated the western mountain plateau, eventually establishing an imamate. Shafis, followers of a major Sunni school of Islam, prevailed along the Red Sea and lowlands south of Sanaa. Geography kept the Sunna and Shi'a separate, preventing much conflict between the groups. But Yemenis also developed greater accommodation than Muslims elsewhere, so Zaidis and Shafis coexisted when their lives intersected.

Yemen's North-South division originated from a treaty between the British and Ottoman empires in 1904. After World War I, a Zaidi imam replaced the Ottomans in the North, but Shafi southerners refused to accept him as religious sovereign, instead strengthening their alliances with the British. The northern Zaidi imams pursued a xenophobic policy that kept their population isolated in high mountain towns and villages. In the South British rule prevailed, and officials used the port city of Aden as a base from which they could loosely supervise traditional rulers in neighboring regions. Later in the mid-twentieth century the British created a federation of sultanates and emirates in South Arabia, but jealousies and rivalries between traditional rulers undermined the system.

This relatively stable if stagnant situation was upset in the 1960s. In 1962 a military coup d'état by pro-Nasser, Arab nationalist officers in the North was followed by a long civil war there. Its settlement in 1967 signaled a conservative tilt to highland Zaidi elites and tribal sheikhs, who remain dominant in the country today. Unrest continued in the North throughout the 1970s and 1980s, with an armed rebellion in the "midlands," a largely Shafi region stretching inland from mountains near the Red Sea to the cities of Ibb and Taiz halfway between Sanaa and Aden. This rebellion was supported by South Yemen, which had gained independence from Britain on November 30, 1967, after a long guerrilla war that began in 1963. Marxists came to power in the South in 1969, and the new regime was so concerned about regional factionalism that it stopped using territorial names, adopting a numerical system for its provinces ("one" through "six") and sub-districts. Yet divisions persisted in the South as they did in the North.

Border disputes between North and South led to war in 1972 and 1979, yet despite these conflicts and the two states' different political orientations, they continued to discuss unification. In the early 1980s they drafted a joint "unity constitution." The process proceeded in fits and starts and was heavily influenced in 1984 by the discovery of oil in the North and in 1986 by internal divisions that weakened the South. Both factors strengthened northern president Saleh's hand during the late 1980s, allowing him to negotiate with the South from a position of strength. Yemen's oil deposits near the North-South border were modest by the standards of the region, but they provided incentives for the South to cooperate in joint exploration. In January 1986 the South's ruling Yemeni Socialist Party (YSP) split, and factional fighting sent President Ali Nasser Muhammad and tens of thousands of supporters fleeing north across the border, where Saleh welcomed them. Saleh played the exiled YSP faction against those who remained in Aden, until reaching a unity agreement with the new southern head of state, Ali Salem al-Beidh, in late 1989. Al-Beidh assured that Ali Nasser Muhammad's partisans were excluded from the deal, and Ali Nasser left for exile in Syria.

North and South Yemen united on May 22, 1990, under a transitional power-sharing formula that attempted to balance political power between

northern and southern officials until the country's first democratic elections. The northern population was, and remains, four to five times larger
than that of the South, so Sanaa became the seat of government while
Saleh served as interim president. The southern YSP leader al-Beidh
accepted the vice president's post. Another southerner from Hadramaut,
Haidar Abdallah al-Attas, became prime minister in charge of cabinet
affairs. The executive authority of government was a five-person body comprising three northerners and two southerners. Thus Saleh clearly held the
swing vote on crucial matters of state policy. Cabinet posts were filled
nearly evenly with northern and southern ministers, each assisted by
deputies from the other side. Despite these arrangements, real unification never took place. Northern and southern officials occupied rival floors
of ministry buildings. Al-Beidh appointed a close associate to be oil minister, but oil revenues were controlled at the ministry of finance, where
Saleh's minister kept the upper hand. The two armed forces were not integrated or placed under a single command, although a few units on each
side were moved across the border. In 1994 these cross-border bases
became flash points of armed conflict that ultimately resulted in a northern military triumph.

The final blow to Yemen's tenuous unity was the political stalemate that
followed the country's first national election on April 27, 1993. The election had been delayed six months because of tensions created by assassinations of southern politicians in Sanaa. Responsibility for the killings was
never clearly established, but rumors ran rampant; those accused ranged
from northern security forces to *mujahideen* returning from Afghanistan
and venting their anti-Soviet anger on former Marxist officials. This danger-
ously charged atmosphere led Yemenis to regard the election as a winner-
takes-all event. But election results were inconclusive.[2]

Saleh's General People's Congress (GPC) gained 40 percent of the seats
in parliament but received only 28 percent of the vote. Islah, a northern
Islamist party whose name means "reform," was the direct descendant of an
Islamic front Saleh created in the 1970s to staunch the spread of southern
Marxist influence; it gained 21 percent of the seats. The YSP placed third,
with 18 percent of the seats and 18 percent of the votes. The remaining
seats were won by independent candidates and small parties. The YSP
swept the polls in the southern districts by landslide margins, affirming its
strength as a regional party. Most GPC and Islah candidates barely won plu-
ralities in hotly contested northern districts. The GPC won the largest share
of parliamentary seats, but it failed to demonstrate its popularity with more

than 80 percent of the population living in the North. The YSP's southern landslide left intact its claim to represent regional interests in the South.

After the election, YSP leaders argued that they had the right to rule the South and proposed a new federal constitutional system with decentralized political power. Northern leaders interpreted any talk of federalism as a plot to secede. Saleh insisted on forming a three-way coalition, with the GPC holding a majority position. But YSP leaders refused to accept anything less than a continued 50-50 share of power with the president's party. The impasse remained until King Hussein of Jordan helped negotiate Yemen's Document of Pledge and Accord (DPA), signed by all parties in Amman in February 1994. Any hopes for peace were short-lived. In late April 1994, fighting broke out at an encampment of southern soldiers near Sanaa. The fighting quickly escalated into full-scale warfare between the armies of the North and South. On May 20, after three weeks of clashes involving Scud missiles lobbed into Sanaa, military aircraft, and heavy artillery, former southern leader Ali Salem al-Beidh formally declared secession. Battles dragged on until July 7, when Saleh's troops marched into Aden while al-Beidh and colleagues fled the country.

The tumult of 1994 reverberates today in the actions of the Southern Movement. Many of its members consider al-Beidh the exiled champion of their cause. Saleh had offered a general amnesty at the end of fighting, but he accused al-Beidh and more than a dozen others of treason. All were tried in absentia, convicted, and sentenced to death, although the sentences were later dropped. Saleh reached out to southerners by promising to decentralize government, as the Amman DPA stipulated, and allow the election of provincial governors and district managers. But most of Saleh's postwar initiatives were calculated to concentrate power in his own hands.

Before the end of the summer in 1994 President Saleh had the unity constitution amended, removing institutions of joint rule and broader distributions of power and granting himself more executive authority to rule by decree.[3] He appointed some southerners, including Vice President Abdul-Rabo Mansour Hadi, to high government posts, but these posts were largely symbolic; lower-ranking northerners served at the president's bidding to prevent any acquisition of independent authority. Saleh also exploited regional and tribal divisions, "dancing on the heads of snakes" as he likes telling visiting journalists, to strengthen his hold on power.[4] At first he relied on the southern "Ali Nasser partisans" who had fled during the 1986 fighting, and whom al-Beidh had excluded at the time of unity. Hadi is from this group, and like Ali Nasser its members primarily originate from Abyan and Shabwa provinces. Later Saleh turned to southern refugees who had fled Marxist rule at the end of the 1960s.

In the weeks following the 1994 war, northern politicians, military officers, tribal sheikhs, and businessmen descended on southern cities, seeking to profit from the defeat of al-Beidh's army. Many northerners occupied the homes of YSP officials who had fled the country. Some southerners talked of the South being "colonized" by the North, yet few offered much resistance; most were too exhausted after eight years of turmoil in their lives. The influx of northerners was followed by the spread of corruption in southern provincial bodies, leading to a perception that the president's family and tribe were enriching themselves on southern resources. Southern lands are less densely populated than those of the North, but they are nearly twice as large and richer in mineral wealth. After unification Yemen's largest oilfield was discovered in Hadramaut province near Ali Salem al-Beidh's home; crude oil production began at al-Maseela field in July 1993. This elevated tensions prior to the 1994 war, and the continued exploitation of southern oil fields remains a source of grievance today. Southerners feel that the wealth generated from their lands is disproportionately distributed to President Saleh's northern military and security forces that are repressing the southern people.

Rise of the Southern Movement

Yemen's unification in 1990 failed to forge a national bond between northerners and southerners. Instead it exposed their divisions, calling into question whether the people form a true nation, with shared social and cultural memories. The project of unity was not helped by an economic crisis that began in the 1990s and grew worse in the next decade. On May 22, 2005, the fifteenth anniversary of unification, President Saleh reached out to southerners by holding the annual unification ceremonies in al-Mukalla, an eastern provincial capital in what had been South Yemen. But only two years later, the Southern Movement burst onto the scene in al-Mukalla and other cities throughout the South with sit-ins, strikes, and demonstrations. The Southern Movement fed on the region's grievances following unification and the war of 1994, and the government's failure to decentralize or expand local government. Saleh's tactics of building patronage with tribes using oil revenues was ill-adapted to the detribalized South. He was further weakened by his close relations with the United States after 9/11, especially during the U.S.-led war in Iraq, which most Yemenis opposed.

After Yemen's 1994 war, the central government dragged its feet on decentralizing power, branding those who pressed for this change as "secessionists" in league with the exiled YSP leaders. It took more than five years for the government to pass its "Local Authority" legislation, and the first local elections were not held until February 2001. Once elected local councils were seated, they were allowed only to consult with the administrators who hold real local authority by appointment of the central government. The councils received inadequate resources to carry out their work, so the experience proved highly disappointing.

By the mid-2000s most citizens in the South had lost trust in Saleh, realizing that he intended to maintain a tight grip on national revenues and policy planning. This loss of trust united the opposition in the southern provinces, where citizens understood that real change would come only through solidarity and protest. Once the Southern Movement's protests began in 2007, the president moved further toward fulfilling his promise of decentralization. In May 2008 he suddenly allowed the indirect election of provincial governors by members of the powerless local councils. But because ordinary citizens were barred from voting, this half-measure failed to placate supporters of the Southern Movement.

The movement gained further momentum because Saleh had exhausted his ability to pit tribe against tribe and faction against faction in the South. After the 1994 civil war, members of Saleh's ruling circle thought they could strengthen their control over the southern regions by pursuing a tribal policy, as they did in the North through their own Hashid tribe. But South Yemen's former Marxist government had detribalized the country in the 1970s. From an early stage, the southern regime criminalized acts of tribal revenge, imposing law and order through an assertion of state power. Traditional sheikhs lost their influence in society, although group loyalties remained in some southern regions.

Tribalism is a stronger factor in the North, where the power of the state is concentrated among members of Saleh's Hashid tribe. The paramount Hashid sheikh was Abdullah Hussayn al-Ahmar, who died at the end of 2007. Prior to unification with the South, Sheikh al-Ahmar served as speaker of the parliament in Sanaa, a post which he resumed as head of the Islah party following the 1994 war. Before and after unification, the most influential northern military and security officers were men from Saleh's family or men from Hashid regions who owed their highest loyalty to Sheikh al-Ahmar. In the late 1990s it seemed that Saleh might build an effective system of patronage in the South based on renewed tribal influence there. But the southern tribal leaders who held the president's confidence soon became disillusioned with his regime. Instead of participating in Saleh's tribal politics, they united with other leading social figures in the South to press greater political demands in Sanaa.

In December 2001 a group of southern dignitaries met in Sanaa throughout the month of Ramadan. They included members of the Yemeni parliament; leaders of political parties, organizations, and tribes; and businessmen. The group—the "Public Forum for the Sons of the Southern and Eastern Provinces"—drafted a letter of complaint to Saleh listing popular grievances in their regions.[5] Its chairman, Ali al-Qufaish, used his long friendship with the president to deliver the group's letter to Saleh's office, thus encouraging a private response. After one month without word, the chairman went public, publishing the group's letter in a widely read newspaper in hopes of forcing the president's hand. Saleh reacted severely, immediately directing government-run media to manufacture scandals about the Public Forum and its chairman. Key southern figures, including tribal sheikhs, understood that neither private nor public appeals would persuade the regime to change. Change would only come through organized opposition.

Saleh's reaction to the Public Forum was severe, but his grasp on power was weakening. Yemenis disapproved of his alliance with the United States following President Bush's declaration of a "war on terrorism." In March 2003 tens of thousand of Yemenis marched on the U.S. embassy when the United States invaded Iraq, and Saleh used deadly force to stop them. Imams across Yemen heaped scorn on the president for standing with American aggression against a fellow Arab Muslim state. Saleh responded with an unprecedented move: ordering police to arrest preachers at mosques, including the Grand Mosque in old Sanaa. Followers of Sheikh al-Houthi's "Believing Youth" organization staged an armed rebellion in Sadah province. The Sadah rebels' success against the government's armed forces—even after their founder was killed in September 2004—inspired southerners, who sensed the time was ripe for mass opposition to the regime.

In May 2007 former southern military officers began holding weekly sit-ins in the streets of cities and towns.[6] These officers had been forced into early retirement after the 1994 war. Their pensions were virtually worthless, so they demanded better compensation. The role of former southern military officers in creating the Southern Movement is significant because the officers symbolize South Yemen's loss of statehood in 1994, when the northern military occupied southern territory. Nasir Ali an-Nuba, leader of the coordinating council for southern military retirees, emphasized the need for peaceful, weapons-free sit-ins. Fearing the spread of opposition, the regime ordered that an-Nuba be arrested along with a few of his colleagues. Protests grew: at first hundreds attended demonstrations, then thousands, and eventually tens of thousands.

A turning point came on the eve of the country's October 14 holiday, which commemorates the start of South Yemen's revolt against British rule in the 1960s. Security forces shot and killed four young men in the same streets where British colonial soldiers had killed seven Yemenis on October 14, 1963. This echo of violence and oppression from more revolutionary times ignited massive anti-government protests across the South, and Saleh was powerless to stop them. In December 2007 hundreds of thousands attended the long-delayed burial ceremony for the four men killed in October. The next month, security forces killed two protesters at an opposition rally in Aden. Less than four months later, government forces killed and injured dozens of southern youths rioting in two southern provinces.

By spring 2008 the anti-government protesters had no central leadership, but they began organizing around the name "Southern Movement," or the "Peace Movement of the South" (*al-Haraka al-Salmiyya lil-Junub*). Multiple groups directed their own local activities. The movement remains decentralized: as recently as January 2010, at least five similarly named organizations each claimed to represent the southern people. When the movement emerged, its senior members called for nonviolence to avoid armed clashes and, above all, to avoid being associated with the jihadists of al-Qaeda or the armed al-Houthi rebels in Saada. Participants at early sit-ins held signs demanding "equal citizenship" and increased powers of local government. By the end of 2008, however, the movement had become radicalized, with protestors demanding "southern independence" and secession.

At rallies in 2009, demonstrators began waving the flag of the former South Yemen, which had not been used publicly since the 1994 war. In early April 2009 Sheikh Tareq al-Fadhli, a former southern ally of Saleh who assisted Saleh's GPC during its showdown with the YSP in the early 1990s, announced that he was joining the Southern Movement. The next month al-Qaeda's leader in Yemen, Nasser al-Wahayshi, declared AQAP's support for the Southern Movement. Al-Fadhli's announcement was more significant because he was quickly welcomed by leaders of the movement inside and outside the country, while the same leaders rejected any association with al-Wahayshi operating from his presumed base in the northern province of Marib. During the South's era of British colonial rule, al-Fadhli's father was an influential sultan. The sultan's family ruled extensive coastal lands east of Aden until all southern property was nationalized under Marxist rule in 1969. President Saleh claimed to restore these nationalized properties after the YSP's defeat in 1994, and the ruling GPC party staked its popularity in the South on a defense of traditional landowning and business interests. Thus Tareq al-Fadhli's break with Saleh in 2009 indicated growing disillusionment among the regime's southern supporters.

In the early 1990s Sheikh Tareq al-Fadhli was very close to Saleh's inner circle. Al-Fadhli's sister married the regime's military strongman, General Ali Mohsin al-Ahmar. More notably, Tareq al-Fadhli is one of the former Arab-Afghan *mujahideen* believed responsible for the 1993 assassinations that, with the regime's consent or support, preceded Yemen's first parliamentary election. Thus Sheikh al-Fadhli's joining the Southern Movement signaled more than a break with Saleh's regime. It also showed the potential reconciliation among southerners who had clashed during the past two decades because of old vendettas from the 1960s. Al-Fadhli now declares his support for an independent southern state led by former YSP leader Ali Salem al-Beidh, previously a villain to the *mujahideen* and traditional landholders among the old southern ruling class.[7]

President Saleh and other top Yemeni officials use Tareq al-Fadhli's support for the Southern Movement to spread fears about al-Qaeda safe havens in restless southern provinces. Al-Fadhli clearly changed the character of the Southern Movement, which grew more belligerent and militaristic after he joined the opposition leadership in 2009. In contrast to the movement's early nonviolent sit-ins, al-Fadhli appeared at public rallies in his hometown Zinjibar of Abyan province with a holstered pistol and heavily armed bodyguards. Questions about Sheikh al-Fadhli and the Southern Movement's relationship with al-Qaeda are more complicated. Leaders of the Southern Movement always reject being associated with al-Qaeda. For his part, al-Fadhli maintains that he fought in Afghanistan during the 1980s alongside local *mujahideen* leaders, not Osama bin Laden.[8] In any case, al-Fadhli is suspected of helping bin Laden and al-Qaeda at a time when he was President Saleh's ally against the regime's opponents in the South. Inside Yemen's regime, General Ali Mohsin al-Ahmar and other key northern figures have as many past ties to religious extremism and terrorism as al-Fadhli.

Whatever alliance Sheikh Tareq al-Fadhli enjoyed with Saleh's regime was shattered in July 2009, when government forces provoked a violent confrontation at the sheikh's home in Zinjibar, killing some of his bodyguards. In reality there are other, more powerful southern sheikhs who are also suspected of ties to al-Qaeda, and many of them support the Southern Movement. But the true problem in the South is not contacts between al-Qaeda and the Southern Movement. It is the unrest created by widespread opposition to the government in Sanaa. This unrest is rooted in Saleh's manipulation of divisions among the southern people and profiteering from southern economic resources. The Southern Movement is fueled by the perception that Saleh's family, which controls Yemen's military and security forces, is siphoning off revenues drawn from local petroleum resources—a significant problem because oil and gas account for roughly 90 percent of Yemen's exports and nearly three-quarters of government revenues.[9]

Dealing With the Southern Movement

The growing talk of secession by Southern Movement leaders raises concerns about Yemen's future and the stability of the Arabian peninsula. If the movement uses more violence in an attempt to secede, Yemen is more likely to become a failed state where extremist groups such as al-Qaeda can thrive. This is why the Southern Movement deserves serious attention by international actors.

The Southern Movement is much more than a security threat linked to al-Qaeda. It is first and foremost a political movement seeking redress for an unsuccessful unification process in the 1990s. Failure to address the underlying problems in the South could further jeopardize security. (Consider Iraq, where al-Qaeda became active only after the 2003 invasion destabilized the country and turned it into a recruiting ground for international terrorism.) Preventing the Southern Movement's transformation into a radical force with strong links to al-Qaeda will require addressing the scars from Yemen's unification and the political problems that fueled the movement's rise. The idea of Yemen as one nation with a shared history has problems: Southerners' experiences before unification were very different from those living in the North, and they remained different in significant ways after 1990. This lack of a unifying narrative makes it difficult to create national unity and bolsters southern opposition to the state. It is important to realize the greater social and political weight behind the Southern Movement because it represents grievances of people who, until very recently, controlled a large territory extending from the tip of the Arab peninsula to the border with Oman. Thus the Southern Movement presents a problem unlike other domestic opposition in the country, and it requires a political—not military or counterterrorism—solution.

Foreign policy makers must think outside the confines of counterterrorism strategy to avoid worsening the situation in Yemen. One of the joint U.S.–Yemeni air assaults in mid-December 2009 that targeted suspected al-Qaeda bases in southern Yemen killed large numbers of women and children in a small village of Mehfed district in Abyan province. Photos of the dead were published online and in newspapers, prompting angry street demonstrations. Southern Movement leaders were quick to reject any ties to al-Qaeda, but participants in the street demonstrations used the bombed village's name as a rallying cry. The United States and other concerned countries must not support Saleh in an expanded military campaign against the Southern Movement. They should push him to address the movement's political grievances, negotiate with southern leaders, address the problem of economic development, and begin the hard process of national reconciliation. Arab leaders should lead this process rather than Western leaders, because Western initiatives, particularly those with a military component, will automatically increase mistrust in the North and South, while raising support for al-Qaeda throughout the country.

The steps toward greater stability in Yemen are clear. Government must grow more transparent and less corrupt. Human rights must be respected, and political opposition must be allowed to organize peacefully. Political prisoners, including the hundreds arrested during street demonstrations in the South, must be released. The government's crackdown on the press must end. Hisham Bashraheel, publisher of the Adeni newspaper *al Ayyam*, was arrested January 4, 2010, after security forces stormed his house. He and dozens of other journalists need international support to gain their release.

The Sanaa government and representatives of the Southern Movement must open talks to arrive at national reconciliation. Exiled former YSP leaders—particularly Ali Salem al-Beidh, Haider al-Attas, and former southern president Ali Nasser Muhammad—should be part of this process because Yemen will remain unstable as long as so many exiled leaders are organizing opposition from beyond the nation's borders. Domestic political opponents must also be included in reconciliation efforts, including southern women who lost social standing after merging with the more conservative North. In 2001 an opposition female candidate named al-Jauhara nearly won the top post on Aden's provincial council. She should be consulted, as should the city's many female professionals like the accomplished lawyer Raqiya Hamaidan.

The reconciliation effort also should include the exiled southern business community and the former southern ruling class. Yemen's economy needs help from successful southern businessmen who prospered in other countries. Prior to the 1994 war, Hadramaut's economy was booming as families who had lived in exile before unification returned, driving up property values. But their plans shifted as the country headed toward conflict. Political processes in the South need to be more inclusive, so southern goals are best served by forming a council of leaders, including former exiles, committed to improving conditions there. That council's work must always be conducted within the framework of a united Yemen, not as a plan for secession. Yet the future structure of the Yemeni state should be open to negotiation during the national reconciliation process.

The Yemeni state is more likely to survive if power devolves from the central government, perhaps in a federal or even confederal system. All international organizations providing aid to Yemen—the World Bank, United Nations Development Programme, United States Agency for International Development, and the UK's Department for International Development—have talked about the need for decentralization, but government resistance to the idea has meant little improvement. In the past year, President Saleh has promised to deepen the process of decentralization by allowing "directly elected local government with broad political powers," a formulation earlier used by the Southern Movement. The international community should seize this opportunity to encourage him to widen the power structure, and it should encourage southern leaders now talking of independence to tone down their rhetoric.

Saleh is one of the Arab world's longest-serving leaders; only the Sultan of Oman and Libya's Colonel Muammar Qaddafi have been in power longer. He must reiterate that he will keep his pledge to leave office when his term ends in 2013, and he must end speculation that he intends to transfer power to someone in his family. (Saleh's son, Ahmed, and three cousins are reportedly being groomed for leadership in the military.) If Saleh were to step down as part of renegotiating Yemen's government structure, and refuse to install a member of his family in his place, it could convince the Southern Movement to drop its secessionist plans.

Such steps will not be easy. There will be resistance by the regime, but also by the most radical elements in the Southern Movement. Complicating matters, the attempt to settle the southern problem by political means will become entangled with ongoing security operations against al-Qaeda and the Houthi rebellion. The success of the political effort in the South will require steady, outside pressure and effective mediation, preferably by an Arab leader like Jordan's late King Hussein, who tried to assist Yemenis in 1994. Ultimately, the success of such an effort will depend on Yemeni leaders on all sides, and their willingness to tackle problems left unsolved since the 1990s.

Notes

1. "In an Unexpected Development: Al-Qaeda's Leader on the Arabian Peninsula Announces His Group's Support for the Southern Movement," *Mareb Press* online, May 13, 2009, http://www.marebpress.net/news_details.php?sid=16554.

2. Abdulaziz Sultan al-Mansoub, *The 1993 Parliamentary Elections in Yemen* (Arabic), Sanaa, Yemen 1995.

3. Stephen Day, "Power-Sharing and Hegemony," Ph.D. Dissertation, UMI Dissertation Services, Ann Arbor, MI, 2001; pp. 379–384. This information will also appear in a forthcoming book by the author, *Yemen Redivided: Twenty Years of Unity Politics in the Era of al-Qaeda.*

4. Victoria Clark, *Dancing on the Heads of Snakes* (New Haven: Yale University Press, forthcoming.)

5. Interview conducted by the author with the Public Forum's director at his home in Sanaa, July 2002.

6. Stephen Day, "Updating Yemeni National Unity: Could Lingering Regional Divisions Bring down the Regime?" *Middle East Journal*, vol. 62, no. 3, Summer 2008; pp. 417–436.

7. "Interview: Al-Fadhli Affirms His Blessings for Ali Salem al-Beidh," *al-Wasat*, May 13, 2009. "Al-Fadhli: The issue is not Yemen's unity for which we paid with our blood, but the South and its well-being," *al-Ayyam*, April 2, 2009, http://www.al-ayyam.info/default.aspx?NewsID=b539f0d3-4903-4b96-80bd-1299c3f9059a.

8. "In His First Press Meeting: Sheikh Al-Fadhli Says He Is Ready to Defend Against Any Accusation of Terrorism," *al-Ayyam*, April 15, 2009, http://www.al-ayyam.info/default.aspx?NewsID=64553a51-9f44-4dc7-8758-80b2f5075527.

9. World Bank, "Country Brief: Yemen," World Bank, http://siteresources.worldbank.org/INTYEMEN/Resources/YEMEN-ENG2009AM.pdf.

WHAT COMES NEXT IN YEMEN? AL-QAEDA, THE TRIBES, AND STATE-BUILDING

Sarah Phillips

News that the attempted Christmas Day bombing of a Northwest Airlines flight to Detroit was tied to al-Qaeda in Yemen brought a flurry of front-page articles warning that the fractious Arab state might become the next Afghanistan. Could al-Qaeda in the Arabian Peninsula (AQAP) bring about the collapse of the fragile Yemeni government and usher in a Taliban-style regime? Is Yemen becoming the next base from which al-Qaeda will target the West?

Western policy makers are scrambling to be seen as responding decisively to the crisis, offering increased military assistance, development aid, or some combination thereof. Foreign intervention presents opportunities for positive change, but there are limits to what it can accomplish. Two issues must inform any action in Yemen: the nature of authority in the state, and the complex relationship between its tribal communities and militant jihadis such as AQAP. Al-Qaeda benefits from the weakness of the Yemeni regime, but the regime's failure would not necessarily be a win for the militants. Yemenis are not inherently sympathetic to militant jihadism, and AQAP probably benefits more from Yemen's position as a weak state than it would if the state were to fail altogether.

The process of state-building in Yemen has been rapid, but remains underway. As recently as fifty years ago, the Yemeni imam presided over a country with no local currency, no sewage system, and only three hospitals.[1] Change has been swift since the republican revolution abolished the imamate in 1962, but the country has never settled on the rules of its political game. As in many developing states, negotiations over "who gets what, when, and how" are ongoing.[2] When a state is in the throes of establishing a new domestic political order, other nations must be more constrained in their involvement there than when it has imploded.

Since Yemen's oil era began in the 1980s, a state-sponsored patronage system has distorted the country's traditional mechanisms of dispute resolution and resource distribution. Tribal sheikhs are pillars in both the traditional and the patronage systems, although in the latter the regime detaches them from their communities by offering wealth and status in exchange for political acquiescence. This has resulted in the rapid centralization of the political system, which was built on the state's capacity to distribute oil wealth to those it deems politically relevant. This centralization, although artificial, has been transformative. Society does not function as it did only one generation ago; today, tribal leaders are rarely the first among equals and are sometimes rather divorced from their tribes' concerns.[3] And, broadly speaking, tribespeople no longer support their sheikhs as tenaciously as they did when the central government enjoyed less power. Now, as the regime's patronage system buckles under the pressure of reduced oil income, its imprint on Yemen's political ecology is clear: The patronage system has eroded many of Yemen's tribal codes and norms, helping create a vacuum where there is no clear alternative to the current patterns of leadership and in which entrepreneurial radicals such as AQAP have greater room to maneuver.[4]

Oil exports are the government's economic lifeline, and still contribute about 75 percent of revenue to the country's national budget. In the six years since Yemen's oil production peaked, extraction has dropped by around 40 percent (to around 280,000 barrels per day), making the country desperately strapped for income. Furthermore, while it is widely reported that Yemen's oil reserves are likely to be depleted by around 2017, the country's oil is also consumed domestically (currently approximately 120–125,000 b/d) and the critical point for the budget is thus even closer than it initially appears. The lack of money in the state's treasury—and the sense of pessimism about the future that this creates—is the most important driver of the country's other political crises.

The Yemeni regime's capacity to contend with domestic challenges such as AQAP has diminished so much in the past two years that by the tenth edition of AQAP's online magazine, *Sada al-Malahim*, in August 2009, AQAP appeared to no longer regard the regime as a significant obstacle to its ambitions.[5] The magazine asserted that AQAP's main goal was now to unseat the regime in Saudi Arabia, noting that Yemeni President Ali Abdullah Saleh's grasp on power was weakening: "We concentrate on Saudi Arabia because the government of Ali Abdullah Saleh is on the verge of collapse [and he is about to] flee the land of Yemen." AQAP's very public assertion that Saleh could not hinder its expansion marks a significant change from earlier editions of the magazine, which had called on Yemenis to fight the regime and hints at AQAP's plans for Yemen. Within a widening political space, AQAP has become more explicit about its domestic political ambitions.

In the same edition of *Sada al-Malahim*, Qassem al-Raymi (one of the founding Yemeni members of AQAP) called for skilled laborers to help "the mujahideen" establish an Islamic state:

> A man's value is in what he does for a living.... The jihadi arena needs all powers, skills and abilities [such as] doctors, engineers and electricians. It also requires plumbers, builders, and contractors, just as it needs students, educators, door-to-door salesmen and farmers. It is searching for media specialists from writers and printers [to] photographers and directors. It is also needs conscientious Muslim reporters and sportsmen, skilled in martial arts and close combat. It is searching for proficient, methodical, organized administrators, just as it is in need of strong, honest traders who spend their wealth for the sake of their religion without fear or greed.
>
> Know my virtuous brother that by following your mujahideen brothers with some of these qualities it will accelerate the pace of achieving our great Islamic project: establishing an Islamic Caliphate. [translated by author]

This is essentially a political manifesto. Al-Raymi is attempting to rally sympathizers to embark on an ambitious state-building project, representative of the pious and directed by the *mujahideen*. AQAP is seeking to destroy the existing political system and establish its own. Much of Yemen's periphery is without effective formal, state-administered governance, but this does not mean that these regions are entirely ungoverned—or there for the taking, particularly by outsiders to the area. The informal norms of tribal governance and authority might have weakened over the past generation, but they remain a powerful local force. If AQAP intends to include Yemen's periphery, where it is currently based, in its political experiment, it must work with the tribes inhabiting those areas. In so doing it will need to remember that tribal communities are motivated by a lot more than religious ideology; one's social responsibility within the tribe is, for example, an often-heard theme in Friday sermons in tribal areas.

In February 2009, AQAP leader Nasser al-Wahayshi and Ayman al-Zawahiri, Osama bin Laden's deputy, demonstrated their understanding that the tribal system is still central to power and authority in large parts of Yemen. Al-Wahayshi called on the tribes to resist pressure to grant the state control of their territory.[6] Likewise, al-Zawahiri called on Yemen's tribes to act like the tribes of Pakistan and Afghanistan and support al-Qaeda:

> I call on the noble and defiant tribes of the Yemen and tell them: don't be less than your brothers in the defiant Pushtun and Baluch tribes who aided Allah and His Messenger and made America and the Crusaders dizzy in Afghanistan and Pakistan... noble and defiant tribes of the Yemen ... don't be helpers of Ali Abdullah Salih, the agent of the Crusaders ... be a help and support to your brothers the Mujahideen.[7]

These statements played on notions of tribal honor, autonomy and, most important, the tribes' long-standing hostility to the central authorities.[8] Clearly al-Qaeda intends to capitalize on the tribes' well-founded distrust of the state.

In September 2009, AQAP released a video discussing the "Battle of Marib" (referring to a recent military operation against AQAP in Marib), which went further in trying to appeal to Yemen's tribal communities. The video's narrator says:

> A lot of excuses were given for this military operation [in Marib] but its main aim was to break the prestige of the tribes and to disarm them. However, the government did not dare to commence its operation until [it secured] a betrayal by some of the sheikhs who allowed the tanks to invade their land.

The state's violence is portrayed as being aimed squarely at the tribes and resulting from tribal sheikhs turning their backs on their responsibilities and traditions. The video then crosses to Qassem al-Raymi, who makes a stinging critique to shame the tribal sheikhs who support President Saleh. He argues that sheikhs who support the president do not represent Yemeni tribes and have lost their legitimacy:

> The biggest shame is for the tribal sheikhs to turn into foot soldiers and slaves of Ali Abdullah Saleh, who is himself a slave to the Saudi riyal and the American dollar. And I say to those sheikhs ... where is

the manhood and the magnanimity ... or did it die with your forefathers and you have buried it with them?

This was a very strong pitch toward notions of tribal honor and the way that a tribal sheikh—and by implication, a tribesman—"should" behave. Al-Raymi is attempting to detach sheikhs who have been co-opted by the state from their tribal support base. He urged the tribes to abandon leaders who had been complicit with the state. These accusations tend to resonate strongly in Yemen's tribal regions, where complaints that the regime has undermined tribal traditions and livelihoods are commonplace. The video's narrator then ties this complaint back to the central goals of al-Qaeda and articulates a central role for Yemen's tribes, saying that the *mujahideen* in Yemen had overcome conspiracies against them because their "unity had increased and the heroes rose swiftly from all the tribes, moved by [their] pure conviction." In this view, the innate heroism of the tribes is aligned with jihadi ambitions to topple the corrupt, irreligious state. The *mujahideen* and the tribes are united. But what would happen if there were no corrupt, irreligious state to combat? Would the alliance that AQAP's leaders seek endure?

What Comes Next?

AQAP is attempting to construct itself as an alternative to a regime that is decried for selectively delivering wealth to Yemen's sheikhs at the expense of their tribes. In so doing it seems to assume an organic acceptance of a jihadi political model within grassroots communities. If al-Raymi's call to establish a new Caliphate is any indication, AQAP also appears to assume that "hearts and minds" are already sympathetic and can be readily converted into viable political institutions. History, most recently in Somalia and Iraq, suggests otherwise.

The growth of localized al-Qaeda groups can present problems when jihadis impose themselves on tribes. As AQAP cells grow stronger, they tend to require more territory for organizing their relationships and operations. The more they require control of territory, the more likely they are to be in competition with the tribes; this is why al-Qaeda groups are unlikely to pose a systemic challenge to the states in which they exist. That changes, however, if the cells are prepared to accept client status of the tribe, as they have partially done in Pakistan. Even if al-Qaeda attempts to discursively and operationally align itself with the Yemeni tribes against the state, one of the group's broader objectives—establishing political control — consigns tribes to a subordinate status. This exclusion would likely put AQAP in confrontation with the tribes.

The desire for political autonomy from a central power is a key component of Yemen's tribal system and the conceptions of honor integral to it.[9] Outsiders might try to break in by offering bounty (money and weapons are standard currencies), or by offering assistance to fight against another outsider to the area. In order to operate effectively in tribally governed territories, outsiders must establish themselves in one of three broad relationships: patrons to the tribe, clients of the tribe, or partners with the tribe.

Patrons to the Tribe

Being a patron to the tribe requires ongoing independent financial largesse from the outsider. Patrons cannot expect their client's loyalty if their ability to pay expires; and sometimes they cannot expect that loyalty even when their largesse continues.[10] In Yemen, the government has attempted to solidify this relationship, but as dwindling oil revenues sap its patronage system, fewer sheikhs are being incorporated or maintained in its networks. The regime is no longer able to offer the benefits it did just five years ago, and the rapid decline is being sharply felt.

Clients of the Tribe

For outsiders operating clandestinely, being the client of a tribe would most likely entail protection, and perhaps logistical assistance, from the tribe in exchange for the outsider playing a spoiler role with the tribe's outside competitors. The value of the outsiders is predominantly their ability to increase the cost of not negotiating with the tribe for other outsiders. This relationship, therefore, requires the subordination of the outsiders to the tribe. Clients can be cast aside, or refused assistance such as safe haven, by their tribal patrons when those patrons no longer see the benefit of maintaining the client.

Some Yemeni tribes appear to be using the threat of al-Qaeda to gain leverage against the state. In October 2008 the government continued negotiations with the Abeeda tribe in Marib in an effort to secure the surrender of al-Raymi. Much of the Abeeda tribe (particularly its major sheikh) are considered pro-government, which suggests that al-Raymi's protection revealed a schism within the tribe itself as some of the more minor sheikhs were offering al-Raymi (and perhaps others like him) refuge to increase their leverage within the tribe against the government or the major sheikh.[11] As the state's patronage system continues to unravel, there is less money available to those on the periphery of that system, which is fueling competition over the depleting resources. Smaller sheikhs are becoming more likely to be cut from the state's largesse and might be more inclined to aid al-Qaeda fugitives to assert their relevance or fill the vacuum created by dwindling state power.

This client relationship hinges on a tenet of Yemeni tribal culture: Honor requires providing hospitality to an outsider who requests protection, and turning over someone who has sought protection is shameful.[12] The tenth edition of *Sada al-Malahim* extolled the duty of sheikhs to give sanctuary to the *mujahideen*, referencing a story of how tribes offered sanctuary to the Prophet during a crisis. Given the cultural imperatives, and the relative inexpense of offering refuge, a tribe's provision of sanctuary does not necessarily mean it would support a more aggressive phase of the *mujahideen's* work. Yemen's government must persuade the tribes that it can offer them more than al-Qaeda can. Al-Qaeda is making the reasonable assumption that the government will not be willing or able to persuade the tribes that it will offer much. They are likely correct, but unlikely to be able to offer much to the tribes themselves.

To most tribes, the Yemeni state is an instrument through which a small band of elites exploits and harasses the people. This will not change unless the state delivers benefits and builds trust between itself and grassroots communities. The Yemeni regime has weakened many aspects of the tribal system by co-opting sheikhs with access to wealth and power from the center, thus severing many from their traditional support bases. Sheikhs now often derive their wealth and status from the political center, rather than their traditional constituency in their local area. With the vacuum of legitimate authority that these fractured center-periphery relationships have created, the Yemeni system is poorly equipped to deal with the political and economic crises it faces. AQAP is presenting its credentials in the regime's stead but is offering little more than a lightning rod for entrenched grievances, of which there are many.

Al-Qaeda's gains in Yemen are rooted in mistakes by the security apparatus and policies that alienate the masses by rewarding the elites. Establishing good governance will be crucial to stability in Yemen, and Western policy makers must not assume the regime is necessarily going to be willing or able to include those it traditionally has excluded.

Partners With the Tribe

A partner relationship with a tribe requires personal, ideological, or goal alignment between the tribe and the outsider. Al-Qaeda groups' internationalist tendencies and exclusive ideology conflicted with local norms in Iraq and Somalia, where tribes valued relative autonomy from a central authority. Yemen is somewhat different in that militant jihadi ideologies had been fostered there decades before jihadis challenged the authority of the state. Thousands of Yemeni nationals returned to the country in the 1980s and early 1990s, following the Soviet war in Afghanistan. Northern elements of the government went to considerable lengths to reintegrate them into Yemen's political life and mobilize them as fighters against the South in the 1994 civil war. Some of these older al-Qaeda affiliates maintain relationships with the government. For younger militants, however—those who came of age during Yemen's oil era—jihadism is not cooperation with the state but resistance to the state.[13]

As Gregory Johnsen points out, AQAP has become a relatively representative organization within Yemen because it is unique among political organizations in its ability to span tribal, regional, and class divisions.[14] Its leaders are reaching out to the tribes, attempting to capitalize on traditional tribal animosity toward the central authorities. However, while widening the cracks in Yemeni society may be achievable, the ability to claim legitimate political and administrative authority does not necessarily follow from this. AQAP is representative in that it has constructed a narrative of popular discontent that has broader reach than other political organizations in Yemen, but it has not demonstrated it can translate this rapport into a palatable political program. Despite its ambitiousness and the relative nuance of its rhetoric, AQAP's presence in Yemen is still fragmented.

Yet AQAP has demonstrated its political sophistication, focusing on the government's injustices and the tribes' need for independence and attaching local Yemeni grievances and cultural sensitivities to its mandate. But the political nature of its goal—"achieving our great Islamic project: establishing an Islamic Caliphate"—and its outsider status are likely to conflict with the tribes' desire to maintain a level of local autonomy. If al-Qaeda hopes to achieve its political objectives in tribal territory, it will have to flex its muscles, and withstand the blowback from that.

This lesson should have been learned in Somalia, where the conflict between al-Qaeda's internationalist ideology and local tribes' demand for autonomy undermined jihadis in the early 1990s. Documents captured by the United States from that time reveal that the foreign *mujahideen* became so exasperated with Somali clan politics that some suggested waging jihad on Somali clan leaders once Western forces had been expelled from the country.[15] In failed states and conflict zones where tribes dominate the political landscape, capable fighters are a much-prized commodity. In Somalia, bin Laden's *mujahideen* could not offer competitive benefits to their most capable potential recruits, many of whom had no desire to put themselves on the wrong side of tribal militias that were deeply suspicious of foreign interference in local affairs.[16]

Such tensions were also important factors in al-Qaeda's reversal of fortune in Iraq's al-Anbar province in 2007–2008, when the tribal "Awakening Councils" paramilitary groups (*al-sahwat*) successfully marginalized the jihadis. Al-Qaeda in Iraq relied on Sunni tribes for support, but went too far in insisting that sheikhs swear an oath to reject tribal legal traditions — a blatant infringement of tribal traditions of autonomy.[17] Al-Qaeda leaders also alienated themselves by attempting to impose themselves in marriage to prominent tribal families, despite cultural norms against women marrying beyond the clan.[18] Al-Qaeda's attempts to wrest control of smuggling networks from the local tribes further aggravated animosity toward these outsiders and undermined an important source of local resource generation for the jihadis.[19] Tribal opposition to al-Qaeda was further galvanized by the jihadis' propensity for using spectacular violence to promote their highly exclusive ideology.[20] Al-Qaeda was an outsider and a competitor that trespassed cultural, political, and economic norms that Iraq's tribes were not prepared to forgo.

Yemen is not Iraq, and the Yemeni regime's historical tolerance of militant jihadis and AQAP's sensitivity to tribal grievances might mean less competition between militants and tribal groups. However, al-Qaeda has relatively little to offer the tribes beyond destructive muscle. It is unlikely to be accepted as a vanguard for the tribes, which could find AQAP's presence a liability.

Violence and Blood Revenge

Al-Qaeda's propensity for extreme violence against civilians will continue to strain its potential support in the Muslim world. In Yemen's tribal society, breaching the peace carries significant consequences: When one tribe kills someone, the tribe of the victim may be entitled to kill "one man of theirs for ours."[21] In the tribal areas, particularly the Marib, al-Jawf, and Shabwa governorates, revenge killings have led to cycles of inter-tribe violence spanning generations and dominating the political and economic landscape—local businesses are disrupted, children can be discouraged from going to school in order to avoid becoming targets, trips to get basic commodities can become dangerous, and so on.

After al-Qaeda's suicide attack against a group of Spanish tourists in Marib in July 2007, the Yemeni government organized a conference in Marib to discuss the causes and solutions to terrorism in the governorate. Marib is highly tribal, and a local tribe was believed to be harboring the al-Qaeda militants who orchestrated the fatal attack. A number of foreign diplomats and NGO employees were invited to attend the conference, and the government assured their security through the use of a mixed tribal escort.[22] In the escort, a member of each of the tribes from surrounding areas sat in the convoy that took the foreigners to and from the conference. Any attack against the convoy would endanger either a member of the tribe that was assisting al-Qaeda or a member of a neighboring tribe, which could spark a blood revenge conflict endangering the attacker's tribe or tribal patron. Tribal society is regulated by complex rules that bind its members to one another. To suggest that it is "ungoverned" overlooks these robust traditions. Mechanisms to maintain a level of stability are intricate and function on the central premise that every individual has an obligation to maintain that stability.[23] These mechanisms are sensitive to outside intervention, particularly when that intervention is predatory. As an external actor with a clear political agenda, AQAP poses a threat to the local mechanisms that maintain a level of order.

Ideology

Ideologically, al-Qaeda might also have difficulties bridging the considerable divides in Yemeni society. In May 2009, al-Wahayshi announced his support for "the people of Southern Yemen" in their struggle to secede from Yemeni President Ali Abdullah Saleh's regime.[24] Although al-Wahayshi's comments were significant, he maintained an explicitly jihadi frame of reference, and emphasized that Islamic law (*shari'a*) was the only way for southerners to overcome the injustices of the regime. Another suspected member of AQAP, Ghalib Abdullah al-Zaidi, added that adopting *shari'a* was necessary for jihadi assistance in the South: "If they *continue* adopting socialist or communist ideas, we will not join them" [italics added].[25] As al-Zaidi's statement suggests, al-Qaeda has ideological competition in the South. Al-Qaeda might have a hard time finding common cause with southern Yemenis if it maintains such a hard-line ideological stance. Yet this stance largely defines al-Qaeda. Cells such as AQAP are becoming more adept at integrating themselves in local political struggles but they do not abandon their internationalist ideology. The traditional Salafi insistence on unity of the *umma* (Islamic community) is inherently at odds with the secessionist movement. AQAP cannot advocate breaks within the *umma* when its mission is the establishment of an international Caliphate. The editorial in issue ten of *Sada al-Malahim* elaborated on this point, denying that AQAP called for political separation in Yemen but pointing out that unified Yemen does not belong to Saleh or former South Yemeni president Ali Salem al-Beidh, whom the article termed "killers."

Marrying internationalist goals and ideology to local concerns is often contradictory. The dialogue between al-Qaeda's internationalist ambitions and the local politics with which its cells become embroiled is strained ideologically and politically. Much of what al-Qaeda stands for is abhorrent to local populations but the exclusion of legitimate opposing voices has created space for extremists like AQAP. Yemenis are religiously conservative, but they are not inherently radicalized. AQAP is providing a narrative of injustice for a population that is suffering, but the jihadis are not (yet) the voice of the people or a surrogate government.

Both al-Qaeda and the Yemeni government have aspirations that clash with those of Yemen's tribes. The gulf between the tribes' local concerns and the internationally focused agenda of al-Qaeda provides opportunities for the government to solve simple grievances and convince the tribes that the government is a better long-term bet than al-Qaeda. However, with the Yemeni regime in crisis, this appears a distant hope. The only long-term solution to the question of bolstering the nation's stability—the regime agreeing to include more of Yemeni society—is unlikely to be achieved soon.

AQAP can ride the wave of local and tribal grievances, but unless it fundamentally alters its ambitions to politically dominate territory in tribal areas—or can demonstrate its capacity to offer tribes tangible and lasting benefits through subordination to al-Qaeda—AQAP is likely to eventually go the way of other outsiders that have attempted the same. This is cause for optimism in the long run; in the short term, projections are much less promising. Yemen's unraveling patronage system gives jihadis a window of opportunity to refine their approach to local politics and entrench themselves as actors in local struggles. Unlike Somalia and Iraq, where al-Qaeda was unable to maintain traction, Yemen is not a failed state. Al-Qaeda benefits from an environment where central authority is weak, but society is not completely chaotic. Experiences in Iraq and Somalia suggest that al-Qaeda groups might be better suited to an environment that is somewhere on the cusp of state failure rather than one in actual failure,[26] and where the prevailing chaos makes jihadis just one group among many fighting for survival. While Yemen's tribal terrain complicates al-Qaeda's ambitions, its chances of becoming perceived as a legitimate political actor increase the longer it functions in the background without overtly challenging the tribes for power.

Addressing the Problem

As the West scrambles to respond to recent events involving Yemen, it is important to consider that neither a military counterterrorism approach nor a short-term developmental approach can correct the source of the problem: The heavily centralized system of power keeps resources and political leverage in the hands of a select few and further entrenches Yemenis' economic hardship.

The growth of militant jihadism in Yemen stems from the malignancy of the country's political system. Targeting AQAP's leadership in Yemen with U.S.-assisted air strikes does not change this, nor is it likely to strengthen the Yemeni regime against militant jihadism in the longer term. The U.S.-assisted air strikes conducted between December 17 and 24, 2009, have been seen on the Yemeni street as an affront to Yemen's sovereignty and were described in some of the local press as massacres. Overt Western military intervention is likely to further entrench AQAP in local political consciousness as the jihadis continue to argue that the Yemeni government is "America's lackey."[27]

The softer "whole of government" approach seems to assume that a loss for the Yemeni regime is a win for al-Qaeda but this oversimplifies the current crisis. A recent policy brief by the Center for a New American Security (CNAS) calls on the U.S. government to "devote even greater resources to ... bolstering the Yemeni government's reach and improving its effectiveness"[28] but this risks further entrenching the problem: More money will not necessarily make the Yemeni regime more willing to genuinely devolve power. The CNAS paper argues that the United States must seek "a multifaceted and enduring relationship that includes economic development, improved government, and domestic stability," pointing out that "less than 20 percent" of the $4.7 billion in aid that was pledged by donors to Yemen in 2006 has been delivered. However, "willingness to follow through with pledges" of aid money[29] is only part of the problem; another significant issue is that the pledged aid cannot be delivered because the arms of the Yemeni government have atrophied and there is no local mechanism through which to effectively deliver such large amounts of aid. This problem speaks volumes about conditions on the ground in Yemen. Unless there is to be an aid mission that intends to perform (and is capable of performing) the basic functions of government, foreign aid needs a local implementing partner. The Yemeni government has not proven it can fulfill this role; historically its leadership has lacked the political willingness and its institutions remain ineffective.

Reinforcing the aspects of the Yemeni regime that threaten its survival is not the answer; a fundamental restructuring of the Yemeni political system is. The system must become far more inclusive, which means removing considerable power from the incumbent elite. This is undesirable in the eyes of some within that elite, particularly those who maintain their influence through extraconstitutional means.[30] At its foundation, this is an issue of leadership, and Yemen needs leaders who are willing and able to catalyze processes of progressive change. The question is whether the West can engage in the intricacies of Yemen's domestic politics without being perceived to underwrite the source of the government's legitimacy problem. This is an enormously complex undertaking and assumes that decisive Western action can engender greater long-term stability in the fragile state. This assumption is based on the long-standing development orthodoxy that foreign technical assistance and structural adjustment can change the nature of domestic political processes. As Yemen's future looks set to become increasingly turbulent, this orthodoxy deserves to be widely debated before being accepted.

Notes

1. William R. Brown, "The Yemeni Dilemma," *Middle East Journal* 17, no. 4, 1963, p. 357.

2. This phrase was popularized by Harold Lasswell in his book *Politics: Who Gets What, When, How* (Cleveland: Meridian Books, 1936).

3. See Paul K. Dresch, "The Tribal Factor in the Yemeni Crisis," in J. al-Suwaidi, ed., *The Yemeni War of 1994: Causes and Consequences* (London: Saqi Books, 1995) p. 40; and Steven C. Caton, *Yemen Chronicle: An Anthropology of War and Mediation* (New York: Hill and Wang, 2005) pp. 331–32.

4. See Sarah Phillips, *Yemen's Democracy Experiment in Regional Perspective: Patronage Pluralized Authoritarianism* (New York: Palgrave Macmillan, 2008); Sarah Phillips, "Politics in a Vacuum: The Yemeni Opposition's Dilemma," *Middle East Institute Viewpoints*, no. 11, June 2009, http://www.mei.edu/Portals/0/Publications/Yemen.pdf; and Sarah Phillips and Rodger Shanahan, "Al-Qa'ida, Tribes and Instability in Yemen," Lowy Institute for International Policy, November 2009, http://www.lowyinstitute.org/Publication.asp?pid=119.

5. The first edition of *Sada al-Malahim* was published in January 2008.

6. Al-Wahayshi's audio speech was posted on various jihadi websites. For English language commentary, see "Al Qaeda Leader Urges Yemeni Tribes to Fight Government," Thaindian News, February 20, 2009, http://www.thaindian.com/newsportal/world-news/al-qaeda-leader-urgesyemeni-tribes-to-fi ght-government_100157355.html.

7. Ayman al-Zawahiri, "From Kabul to Mogadishu," statement released February 22, 2009, http://www.nefafoundation.org/miscellaneous/FeaturedDocs/nefazawahiri0209-2.pdf.

8. Brian O'Neill, "AQAP a Rising Threat in Yemen," *CTC Sentinel*, 2(4): 17–19, 2009, http://www.ctc.usma.edu/sentinel/CTCSentinel-Vol2Iss4.pdf.

9. See Steven C. Caton, *"Peaks of Yemen I Summon": Poetry as Cultural Practice in a North Yemeni Tribe* (Berkeley and Los Angeles: University of California Press, 1990) pp. 31–2; Paul K. Dresch, *Tribes, Government and History in Yemen* (Oxford: Clarendon Press, 1989) pp. 47, 378; and Manfred W. Wenner, *The Yemen Arab Republic: Development and Change in an Ancient Land* (Boulder, CO: Westview Press, 1991) pp. 39–40.

10. The literature on tribes in Yemen is full of anecdotes about tribes that were "republican by day, and royalist by night," in the 1960s northern civil war. The kaleidoscopic nature of shifting tribal alliances is often baffling to an outsider. Robert Stookey quotes a combatant in that war who had attempted to purchase the allegiance of tribesmen: "One had deserted because the republicans had bought him off; the other went off and attacked on his own, elsewhere than had been expected, because he was suspicious. That's the way it has always been." See Robert W. Stookey, *Yemen: The Politics of the Yemen Arab Republic* (Boulder, CO: Westview Press, Inc., 1978) p. 244.

11. Interview with Yemeni analyst of tribal politics, Sanaa, October 2008.

12. Dresch, *Tribes, Government and History in Yemen*, pp. 64–5.

13. Gregory D. Johnsen discusses the generational split in more detail in "Al Qaeda's Generational Split," *Boston Globe*, November 9, 2007, http://www.boston.com/bostonglobe/editorial_opinion/oped/articles/2007/11/09/al_qaedas_generational_split.

14. Gregory D. Johnsen, "Waning Vigilance: Al-Qaeda's Resurgence in Yemen," Washington Institute for Near East Policy, Policy Watch no. 1551, July 14, 2009, http://www.washingtoninstitute.org/templateC05.php?CID=3088.

15. Combating Terrorism Center (CTC) at West Point, *Al-Qa' ida's (Mis)Adventures in the Horn of Africa*, West Point, NY: U.S. Military Academy, 2006, http://www.ctc.usma.edu/aq/pdf/Al-Qa%27ida%27s%20MisAdventures%20in%20the%20Horn%20of%20Africa.pdf, p. 6.

16. Ibid., pp. 16–18.

17. Peter Bergen et al., "Beyond Iraq: The Future of AQI," in *Bombers, Bank Accounts and Bleedout: Al-Qa' ida's Road in and out of Iraq*, B. Fishman, ed. West Point, NY: U.S. Military Academy, 2008, http://www.ctc.usma.edu/harmony/pdf/Sinjar_2_July_23.pdf, p. 114.

18. Andrew Phillips, "How al Qaeda Lost Iraq," *Australian Journal of International Affairs*, 63(1): 64–84, 2009, p. 72.

19. Ibid.

20. Ibid., p 73.

21. Dresch, *Tribes, Government and History in Yemen*, pp. 50–51, 66–69, 150.

22. The author attended this conference.

23. It is important to note that while the attempt to foster stability through deterrence is not always effective—and mediation is an important part of resolving disputes that have occasioned death—the impact on the local environment is very serious when it fails, and the possibility of this is not taken lightly.

24. Arafat Madayash and Sawsan Abu-Husain. "Al Qaeda Call for Islamic State in Southern Yemen," *Asharq Alawsat*, May 14, 2009.

25. "Al-Qaeda: we'll help southerners if they rule with Islamic laws," News Yemen, May 19, 2009, http://www.newsyemen.net/en/print.asp?sub_no=3_2009_05_19_7760.

26. Thanks are owed to Gavin Hales for articulating this point in email correspondence.

27. "Qaeda makes rare public appearance at Yemen rally," Reuters, December 21, 2009, http://www.reuters.com/article/idUSTRE5BK3YF20091221.

28. Andrew M. Exum and Richard Fontaine, "On the Knife's Edge: Yemen's Instability and the Threat to American Interests," Policy Brief, Center for a New American Security, 2009, http://www.cnas.org/files/documents/publications/yemen_Policy_Brief_0.pdf, p. 5.

29. Ibid.

30. I thank Abdul-Ghani al-Iryani for this phrase.

STABILIZING A FAILING STATE

Marina Ottaway and Christopher Boucek

The preceding analytical essays on Yemen, written by authors with extensive field research experience in the different regions of the country, converge toward strikingly similar conclusions: Yemen today is a state at risk of failure not because it has been targeted by a single, coordinated assault on its survival, but because it faces a set of disparate threats, each resulting from an accumulation of specific grievances with different causes. Al-Qaeda in the Arabian Peninsula, the Houthi rebels, the Southern Movement, and even some tribes oppose the government and literally are up in arms against it for their own distinct political reasons. True, the unrest is taking place against a background of dire socioeconomic conditions, but each organization's specific grievances and demands are helping that discontent coalesce into a movement.

The Southern Movement and the Houthi rebels have their own, somewhat parochial, goals. Even al-Qaeda in the Arabian Peninsula (AQAP), whose narrative of government wrong-doings and proposed solutions in theory transcends local and national considerations, has been unable to build a broad-based movement. Whether AQAP has 300 or 3,000 members matters when designing an effective counterterrorism strategy, but politically it is of scant importance: Both numbers show that AQAP has limited support. The parochial concerns and differences among opposition groups that prevent a unified movement from emerging are a good thing for the Yemeni government, which probably could not withstand a coordinated attempt at destabilization from all dissatisfied groups in the country. These groups' competing demands also make it difficult to devise a unified strategy to stabilize Yemen.

Any attempt to deal with the root causes of the political violence that threatens Yemen needs to recognize the disparate nature of the various movements and to address their specific demands. This is a complex, highly political effort that requires an intimate knowledge of each situation and of the groups and individuals driving the opposition. Devising such an approach is difficult; implementing it will be even more so. As a result, international efforts at stabilizing Yemen appear to draw more on the generic ideas about how to deal with states at risk and on the general prescriptions of counterterrorism efforts than on the specifics of each crisis that threatens Yemen's stability. This will certainly limit the effectiveness of the efforts.

The danger of state failure in Yemen, with the resulting political and humanitarian consequences, is of grave concern to the international community and most directly to Yemen's neighbors in the Arabian Peninsula. The Gulf states would bear the brunt of humanitarian disaster and instability across their borders, as well as face most directly the threat posed by ungoverned territories. As a result, there is broad agreement in Europe, the United States, and the Gulf that state failure in Yemen cannot be tolerated, and that the country must be stabilized. The question is whether outside intervention, particularly by Western countries whose actions in the Middle East are always controversial, can help the country stabilize without creating a backlash that could bring disparate organizations closer together.

Intervening in Fragile or Failing States: The General Approach

Bilateral donors and multilateral agencies have developed prescriptions for avoiding state failure. Support and assistance from Western countries, and to an extent from neighboring Arab countries, conforms closely with these plans and with counterterrorism approaches as the global community works to prevent failure in Yemen.

Interventions to stabilize states at risk have become relatively common since the end of the Cold War. As a result, international organizations and bilateral aid agencies have made serious attempts to codify their approaches to stabilization and to harmonize with those of other concerned actors. The United Nations, the World Bank, and the Organisation for Economic Co-operation and Development (OECD) all have produced documents outlining an approach to what are variously called failing, failed and fragile states, or states at risk, and so have aid agencies in the United States, the United Kingdom, and other major OECD countries. The prescriptions set forth in such documents represent a distillation of lessons learned from past interventions; this is a positive development. On the negative side, however, codified approaches are general by definition and do not address the specific problems of each situation. In fact, while most agencies acknowledge that interventions in failing states require an analysis of the political situation, the analysis is often shortchanged; programs are designed to address basic development issues rather than political grievances. For Yemen, where the danger of collapse stems from the convergence of a number of problems, each with a different dynamic, addressing the common denominator of poverty and poor governance might not be enough.

Prescriptions for dealing with failing states share several basic, common assumptions.[1] First, the goal of intervention is not to restore the security and the stability of the state per se, but to restore stability so that the state can provide for the security of its citizens. The ultimate goal is human security, not state security—although in practice state security is seen as a precondition for human security. Interventions, as a result, always aim at restoring the capacity of existing states. The authors are not aware of any case where the international community accepted, let alone recommended, the dissolution of a state in the name of human security. For example, the only part of Somalia that has provided a minimum of security to its population in the past twenty years, Somaliland, has not received recognition, while considerable effort has been devoted to the Sisyphean task of restoring the Somali state to its old borders. There are sound political reasons for this preference for restoring the security of existing states, although the preference is not always beneficial to human security.

Second, while in some cases restoring stability requires military intervention or, as in Yemen, assistance to the country's security forces, such interventions are seen just as a first step—necessary but not sufficient. Unless the government becomes more willing and capable of addressing the social and economic problems that affect the everyday lives of citizens, people will remain disaffected and open to supporting even violent opposition groups.

Third, addressing social and economic problems requires both fundamental reforms and the implementation of fast disbursing projects that can quickly and tangibly improve citizens' lives by creating employment, increasing food and water availability, promoting women, putting children in schools, and addressing at least basic health issues.

Fourth, it is crucial that countries and agencies seeking to stabilize fragile and failing states coordinate and harmonize their policies so different actors will not work at cross purposes. This is a completely non-problematic prescription in theory, but it chronically falls short in implementation.

These ideas—a quick summary of the documents on fragile and failing states from international organizations and bilateral agencies—are very similar to the prescriptions of counterterrorism experts. They agree that the fight against extremist groups can never be won simply by military means, so all programs to fight terrorism should include a development component. The idea that counterterrorism encompasses more than security measures is hardly new, but it has received renewed attention recently as part of the interventions in Iraq and Afghanistan. The early 2010 operation by U.S. and Afghan troops in Marjah and the surrounding region in southern Afghanistan is a good example of the application of this approach: The military advance is expected to be followed by a massive effort to bring governance to a long-neglected region. In theory, this should restore the population's confidence in the central government and make it less inclined to support or tolerate the Taliban's presence and its control.

The broad consensus on what needs to be done to stabilize failing states should not lead to complacency. There is no doubt that everybody is on the same page, but is it the right page? Do interventions to stabilize failing states work? Is there a better approach?

Irrespective of whether the approach can be improved, or that a different approach would simply trade one set of problems for another, it has become clear from the experience of many interventions that stabilization efforts have many shortcomings, some of which appear particularly relevant in the case of Yemen. Programs to address socioeconomic problems in countries at risk of failure are inevitably inadequate. The problems are immense, state capacity is by definition minimal, and funding never is sufficient. The usual answer—that responses should focus on the most strategic interventions, those with the greatest multiplier effect—is obvious in theory. However, in practice it never is obvious which measures have the greatest strategic value in a particular situation. As a result, all too often socioeconomic interventions end up as a hodgepodge of separate projects.

Similarly challenging is the lack of state capacity to implement policies. The more fragile the state is, and thus the lesser its implementing capacity, the greater the probability that international NGOs will be in charge of implementing socioeconomic assistance projects. This outside intervention in turn undermines the government's own capacity. This is a problem that occurs regularly in failing states and for which there is no simple solution.

Another serious problem that always emerges is the disparity between the immediacy of the crisis and the long-term character of most socioeconomic interventions considered crucial to stabilization. Addressing economic problems takes time. Improving services takes time. Again, the theoretical answer is simple: Agencies intervening in failing states should focus initially on reforms that will have an immediate impact—so-called zero-generation reforms—and on quick-disbursing projects. In practice, there are very few such reforms, and the only truly quick-disbursing projects are humanitarian interventions.

The conclusion is not that socioeconomic reforms and projects should not be undertaken in failing states. These efforts are badly needed, and the sooner that work starts the better it will be for the country—assuming that international attention can be maintained for the long run. But it is not enough. In addition to the security measures needed in most cases to stabilize failing states, and the long-term socioeconomic interventions necessary to address the fundamental problems afflicting all failing states, there is another layer of steps that need to be undertaken: addressing the political grievances that are the most immediate, proximate cause of the development of radical, destabilizing movements. In Yemen, the division between North and South is not going to be bridged by security measures and economic programs alone; it must also be bridged by political measures including negotiations. Political interventions are the most difficult task for the political community; they are prone to back-firing, and the temptation to neglect them is always considerable. Socioeconomic assistance appears much safer.

Theory Meets Reality: The Emerging Approach in Yemen

Many of the typical problems afflicting interventions to stabilize failing states are becoming quite evident in the case of Yemen. Despite an attempt to bring together all donors in a concerted effort to address security and development simultaneously, considerable problems are beginning to surface. Coordination is lagging, and different countries' programs appear to depend on national choices rather than an overall plan. The United States is focusing almost exclusively on security in the narrow terms. The United Kingdom is more focused on economic issues; it has the largest program among Western donors, but this program has insufficient funds to make a fundamental difference. Saudi Arabia, by far the largest aid provider in

Yemen, does not appear to have a clear plan other than keeping the country afloat. International agencies preach economic reform with marginal success. And nobody is really addressing political grievances, least of all the government, whose task it really should be.

There remains a considerable gap in Yemen between the theory of what intervention in fragile states should accomplish and the reality of what is happening. The major challenges for the international community in Yemen are to recalibrate the balance between security and socioeconomic assistance and to convince the Yemeni government to start addressing the most fundamental grievances that give armed movements a following.

None of this is going to be easy. First of all, terrorism and security fears are the reason why the United States, European countries, and regional states are currently involved in Yemen. Indeed, the level of interest in Yemen and the sense of urgency in addressing the country's problems tend to wax and wane depending on the current threat perception. The attempt on Christmas Day 2009 by a young Nigerian trained in Yemen to set off a bomb on an airliner as it was landing in Detroit heightened U.S. interest in Yemen for a while, but the sense of urgency has already decreased. Second, the problems that make Yemen a state on the brink are not easily addressed. As all the chapters in this volume show, the ultimate threat to the Saleh regime's ability to effectively govern and exercise control over Yemen is not a few hundred or even thousand armed men in different parts of the country. Rather, Yemen's stability is most threatened by systemic issues: governance that is insufficient in quantity and quality, corruption, resource depletion, and lack of development. The challenges posed by AQAP, the war in Saada, the Southern Movement, and increasingly restive tribes are not the cause of Yemen's fragility, but the result of a potent combination of both declining state capacity and legitimacy and the regime's decreasing responsiveness to the population. Third, donors' efforts are both limited and poorly coordinated. As much as the international donor community needs better coordination, the Yemeni government must learn to better manage the international donor process.

In the immediate aftermath of the attempted Christmas Day bombing, British Prime Minister Gordon Brown called an international meeting to address Yemen's growing problems and their impact on global security. The British government was well-placed to call the meeting: Yemen has been a priority in its assistance program for years, and Britain just emerged from a year-long policy review. At the January meeting, the British argued the need to improve the Yemeni state's capacity to maintain domestic security while taking on pressing political and economic reforms. U.S. Secretary of State Hillary Clinton echoed this sentiment by urging the international community to view Yemen not only through a "counterterrorism prism" but also as a social and economic challenge. At least on paper, participants in the meeting heeded the call for a broad approach and for coordination. The twenty countries participating set up a "Friends of Yemen" group designed to bolster international support and streamline foreign assistance. They also created two working groups: one, spearheaded by the Germans and Emiratis, focused on economic and governance issues; the other, under Dutch and Jordanian leadership, on justice and rule of law issues. This approach was heralded as a means to improve international coordination, but the process has yet to deliver results.

The January meeting was purposefully designed not to be a donors' conference, but rather to be a forum for facilitating the coordination and delivery of international assistance, which previously had been unsatisfactory. A donors' conference in 2006, for example, raised just over $5 billion in pledges, but more than 80 percent was never disbursed because of a range of concerns, including how the funds would be used. In addition to seeking to improve coordination, the January conference also sought to broaden the circle of concerned countries. A major development in this respect was the decision of the Gulf Cooperation Council to participate in the Friends of Yemen process. Saudi Arabia and other GCC countries have been by far the largest financial supporters of Yemen. Their continuing involvement, and better coordination between them and other countries, is essential to the success of stabilization efforts.

The January summit was followed in late February by a technical coordination meeting of the Friends of Yemen in Riyadh. Intended to focus on technical issues, the meeting highlighted real problems in the relationship between the Yemeni government and the donors. For Yemeni officials, the main concern was to increase the flow of assistance and to make sure that countries would deliver on their pledges. They pressed for direct budgetary assistance and were anxious to know how the Friends of Yemen would deliver funds. Yemenis also pressed the Gulf countries to admit more Yemeni workers in order to ease the pressure of unemployment. But donors, while recognizing that Yemen needed help, worried about its government's capacity to manage the funds and deliver on the technical requirements. In general, the Riyadh meeting showed the need for much improvement in the communications between the Yemeni government, which must understand the donors' need to know that funds will be well and honestly managed, and the donors, who must accept that Yemen needs help now and that they cannot wait until the country develops greater management capacity.

The meetings have resulted in a substantial increase in the pledged assistance as well as involvement in the reform process. Multilateral organizations, such as the United Nations, International Monetary Fund, World Bank, and European Union are increasingly active in pushing the government to enact immediate economic reforms. Among Western donors, the United Kingdom remains the largest, spending £27.5 million in FY 2009–2010. Germany has also boosted funding, concentrating on humanitarian relief for internally displaced persons in the areas affected by fighting in Saada.

Western countries and international organizations have been the most vocal in these meetings, particularly in their advocacy of reform, but the Gulf countries are keeping Yemen afloat. The United Arab Emirates, driven by fears that rising instability in Yemen would have a dire domestic impact, announced a funding package in excess of $600 million, with a focus on projects related to education, infrastructure, and water issues. The crucial country, however, is Saudi Arabia, by far Yemen's largest funder.

Although it is extremely difficult to accurately assess the total of the gifts and grants, formal and informal, comprising Saudi assistance to Yemen, rough estimates put it between $1.75 billion and $2 billion per year. No other country comes even close to this level of financial commitment or has similarly extensive ties to Yemen. Because of the deep linkages between the two countries—their history, culture, economic exchanges, and labor migration—Yemen policy in the Kingdom is very much a domestic rather than foreign policy issue. Indeed, Yemen policy in Saudi Arabia is not controlled by the Foreign Ministry but is the personal portfolio of Crown Prince Sultan. Saudi Arabia's deep involvement in Yemen earns it a pivotal role in any evolving strategy to stabilize Yemen. Unfortunately, Saudi Arabia does not appear to have a single, well-articulated policy toward Yemen. Rather, many actors within the Kingdom have financial and patronage ties to a range of Yemeni organizations, individuals, and groups. The absence of a well-delineated Saudi policy, with clear lines of control and leadership, complicates any international or regional approach to stabilizing Yemen. Maintaining alignment between Western and Saudi interests and goals in Yemen will require extensive coordination and a deeper understanding of what Riyadh ultimately wants to see in Yemen.

U.S. assistance to Yemen deserves a separate discussion, because the United States has overwhelmingly focused on military and security assistance. Publicly available figures suggest that U.S. economic and humanitarian assistance will increase with the next budget from $20 million to $50 million, and military and security assistance will rise from $60 million to $150 million. (All these figures are approximate.) This represents a dramatic increase following the 1990 Gulf War when aid to Yemen was cut to almost zero. This approach, however, risks "securitizing" the situation in Yemen. As Barbara Bodine, former U.S. ambassador to Sanaa, points out, the military and security services are not the strongest institutions in Yemen, and we should be careful not to elevate such organizations too much.

The American policy priority vis-à-vis Yemen is counterterrorism narrowly defined, as shown by the three-to-one ratio of military aid to economic aid. The priority also is reflected in the fact that several months on from the Christmas Day attack, the United States has not put any pressure on Yemen to address seriously the systemic problems of governance, corruption, lack of economic development, or resource depletion that threaten the future of Yemen. Nor has the United States pressured Yemen to address the political grievances that fuel the armed opposition. As all essays in this collection highlight, these are the most severe challenges facing the Yemeni government. If left unaddressed, they will be the issues that likely will lead to state collapse.

The international effort to prevent Yemen from going over the brink has many shortcomings: the United States' choice to deal with Yemen almost exclusively as a security issue; the lack of clarity in the Saudi policy; the disparity between the country's need for reform and investment in all sectors and the limited financial and human resources; and the eternal problem of insufficient donor coordination. But it is also important to consider that donors cannot stabilize Yemen without the cooperation of its government, and that many of the reforms that Yemen needs to implement are seen by many in the Yemeni governing elite as direct challenges to the current system and their personal positions. This poses a true dilemma for donors, who have chosen to include the Saleh government as a partner in improving the security and stability of the country. Indeed, the international community should not be working against the Yemeni government. But measures that are in the long-term interest of the country are not necessarily in the short-term interest of incumbents. Without strong pressure to address the systemic challenges facing the country, it is extremely doubtful that the Yemeni government will make any serious efforts to curb corruption, improve governance, or address political grievances, which are directed against the government itself. As long as donors remain divided, there can be no such pressure on the government of Yemen.

Note

1. Among the many documents, see World Bank, *Engaging with Fragile States* (Washington, D.C.: World Bank, Independent Evaluation Group, 2006). The report also contains the Principles for International Engagement in Fragile States published by the Development Assistance Committee of the Organisation for Economic Co-operation and Development. U.S. Agency for International Development, *Fragile States Strategy*, 2005. UK Department for International Development, *Why We Need to Work More Effectively in Fragile States*, 2005. See also Louise Andersen et al., eds., *Fragile States and Insecure People?: Violence, Security and Statehood in the Twenty-First Century* (New York: Palgrave Macmillan, 2007).

INDEX

Abdulmutallab, Umar Farouk, 31
Abeeda tribe, 80–81
Abyan (governorate), 37–38, 66, 70
Aden (city), 7, 62–63, 69, 72
Afghanistan
    anti-Soviet jihad in, 12–13, 64, 70, 82
    counterterrorism and, 23
    lawlessness in, 3, 75
    terrorism in, 15, 17, 39
    tribalism in, 78
    U.S. war against, 94
Agriculture, 22
al-Ahmar, Abdullah Hussayn, 67
al-Ahmar, Ali Mohsin, 70
al-Aidroos, Amir Salem, 4
al Ayyam (newspaper), 72
al-Farhan tribe, 54
al-Haqq party, 51
al-Haraka al-Salmiyya lil-Junub (Peace
    Movement of the South), 69
al-Qaeda in the Arabian Peninsula (AQAP)
    al-wala' wal-bara' tenet, 37
    analysis of, 42
    assessment of threat from, 36–37
    attraction to, 36–37
    counter-radicalization efforts aimed at,
      41
    demographics of, 33
    developmental approach to, 40–41

    diagnostic framework of, 36–37
    difficulty in subverting existing states,
      79–80
    economic factors in attraction to, 40–41
    evolution of, 32, 34–35
    exaggeration of threat from, 38
    failing state, contribution to, 91
    foreign fighters and, 39–40
    generally, vii–viii, 31–32
    governorates, support for in, 38, 41–42
    hard power approach to, limitations of,
      40–41
    human rights and, 41–42
    ideology, unpopularity of, 84–86
    law enforcement response to, 41–43
    media of, 33
    military response to, 41–42
    political shortcomings of regime
      strengthening, 86–87
    prognostic framework of, 37–38
    recommendations re, 41–43
    regional approach to, 43
    resurgence of, 12–15
    Saada insurrection and, 37
    safe haven in Yemen for, 39–40
    Saleh, on, 77–79, 85
    Saudi Arabia and, 14, 32, 33, 40, 43, 77
    southern secessionist movement and,
      62, 69–71, 73–74

CONTRIBUTORS

CHRISTOPHER BOUCEK is an associate in the Carnegie Middle East Program, where his research focuses on regional security challenges. Before joining the Carnegie Endowment, he was a postdoctoral researcher at Princeton University and lecturer in Politics at the Woodrow Wilson School. He was also previously a media analyst at the Royal Embassy of Saudi Arabia in Washington, D.C., and worked for several years at the Royal United Services Institute for Defence and Security Studies in London, where he remains an associate fellow. From 2003 to 2005, he was a security editor with Jane's Information Group. Boucek has written widely on the Middle East, Central Asia, and terrorism for a variety of publications including the *Washington Post, CTC Sentinel, Jane's Intelligence Review, Journal of Libyan Studies, Strategic Insights,* and *Terrorism Monitor.*

STEPHEN DAY is an adjunct professor at Rollins College in Winter Park, Florida, and he also has taught at Stetson University in central Florida and St. Lawrence University in New York. He is the author of "Updating Yemeni National Unity: Could Lingering Regional Divisions Bring down the Regime?" *Middle East Journal,* Summer 2008 and a forthcoming book entitled *Yemen Redivided: Twenty Years of National Unity in the Era of Al-Qaeda.*

ALISTAIR HARRIS is a former diplomat and UN staff member. He is an associate fellow at the Royal United Services Institute (RUSI) and frequent commentator for RUSI on Middle Eastern issues, as well as director of the research consultancy Pursue Ltd. A specialist in counter-radicalization, security sector assistance, and post-conflict stabilization, he has worked in recent years in the Balkans, Pakistan, Afghanistan, Yemen, the Palestinian Territories, Lebanon, and Africa. Harris has a first class degree from Emmanuel College, Cambridge, and is a graduate student at the Centre for the Study of Terrorism and Political Violence at St. Andrews University.

MARINA OTTAWAY is the director of the Middle East Program at the Carnegie Endowment for International Peace. She works on issues of political transformation in the Middle East and of Gulf security. A long-time analyst of the formation and transformation of political systems, she has also written on political reconstruction in Iraq, Afghanistan, the Balkans, and African countries. Before joining the Endowment, Ottaway carried out research in Africa and in the Middle East for many years and taught at the University of Addis Ababa, the University of Zambia, the American University in Cairo, and the University of the Witwatersrand in South Africa. Her most recent book, *Getting to Pluralism*, co-authored with Amr Hamzawy, was published in 2009.

SARAH PHILLIPS lectures at the Centre for International Security Studies, Sydney University. She lived and worked in Yemen for nearly four years and specializes in Middle Eastern politics and the politics of state-building. Her recent book *Yemen's Democracy Experiment in Regional Perspective* (2008) was published by Palgrave Macmillan. Small sections of her chapter were published by the Lowy Institute for International Policy in "Al-Qa'ida, Tribes and Instability in Yemen" (with Rodger Shanahan), 2009.

Carnegie Endowment for International Peace

THE CARNEGIE ENDOWMENT FOR INTERNATIONAL PEACE is a private, nonprofit organization dedicated to advancing cooperation between nations and promoting active international engagement by the United States. Founded in 1910, its work is non-partisan and dedicated to achieving practical results.

Following its century-long practice of changing as global circumstances change, the Carnegie Endowment is undertaking a fundamental redefinition of its role and mission. Carnegie aims to transform itself from a think tank on international issues to the first truly multinational — ultimately global — think tank. The Endowment has added operations in Beijing, Beirut, and Brussels to its existing centers in Washington and Moscow. These five locations include the two centers of world governance and the three places whose political evolution and international policies will most determine the near-term possibilities for international peace and economic advance.